101 Database Exercises

(For dBASE III Plus, Lotus® 1-2-3, and Other Database Management Systems)
Second Edition

Jeffrey R. Stewart

Professor of Business Education
Virginia Polytechnic Institute and State University
Blacksburg, Virginia

Sandra R. McMinnis

Instructor in the School of Business Administration
The Pennsylvania State University, Capital Campus
Harrisburg, Pennsylvania

Nancy M. Melesco

Senior Computer Programmer Analyst
Comdial Corporation
Charlottesville, Virginia

GLENCOE

Macmillan/McGraw-Hill

Lake Forest, Illinois
Columbus, Ohio
Mission Hills, California
Peoria, Illinois

101 Database Exercises
(For dBASE III Plus®, Lotus® 1-2-3, and Other Database Management Systems), Second Edition

dBASE III Plus is a registered trademark of Ashton-Tate Corporation.
Lotus 1-2-3 is a registered trademark of Lotus Development Corporation.

Send all inquiries to:

GLENCOE DIVISION
Macmillan/McGraw-Hill
936 Eastwind Drive
Westerville, OH 43081

ISBN-0-02-800748-4

Printed in the United States of America.

1 2 3 4 5 6 7 8 9 POH 99 98 97 96 95 94 93 92 91

Contents

About the Authors _____ vi

Introduction _____ vii

Exercise	Title	Page

▼ **FAUNTEROI'S CUSTOMER FILE**

	Unit I – Faunteroi's Customer File _____	1
1A	Indexing Names of Individuals _____	3
1B	Indexing Personal Names With Prefixes _____	5
2A	Indexing Names With Titles and Suffixes _____	7
2B	Indexing Hyphenated Personal Names _____	9
2C	Optional Indexing Exercise—Indexing Customer Names, Forms 001 Through 036 _____	10
3	Creating the File _____	11
4	Keying Data From Forms 001 Through 036 _____	12
5	Listing Customer Names and Account Numbers ____	12
6	Proofreading Your Listing _____	13
7	Helping the Accountant _____	14
8	Finding the Customers _____	15
9	Adding New Customers _____	15
10	Updating Records _____	15
11	Printing Mailing Labels _____	16
12	Printing a Customer Report _____	16
13	Answering Phone Inquiries _____	17
14	Deleting Records _____	17
15	Listing Paid-Up Customers _____	18
16	Checking Credit Limits _____	18
17	Modifying the Database Structure and Updating Records _____	19
18	Adding More New Customers _____	19
19	Answering More Inquiries _____	20
20	Reporting Preferred Customers _____	21
21	Test—Faunteroi's _____	21

▼ **QUANTUM CORPORATION EMPLOYEE FILE**

	Unit II – Quantum Corporation Employee File _____	37
22	Creating the File _____	39
23	Inputting Data From Forms 001 Through 028 _____	40
24	Listing the Entire File _____	40
25	Searching the File _____	41
26	Listing Hourly Employees in the Research Department _____	41
27	Adding New Employees _____	42
28	Making Some Changes _____	42
29	Finding the Salaried Employees _____	42
30	Answering Inquiries _____	43

		Exercise Title	Page

QUANTUM CORPORATION EMPLOYEE FILE
Continued

Exercise	Title	Page
31	Finding Wage Information	43
32	Reporting Names of Employees Nearing Retirement	44
33	Changing Records	44
34	Deleting Records	44
35	Making More Changes	45
36	Adding New Employees	45
37	Listing Research Department Employees	45
38	Finding an Employee	46
39	Reporting Employees by Department	46
40	Reporting the Sales Employees	47
41	Changing Job Titles	47
42	Listing Research Associates	47
43	Reporting All Employees by City	48
44	Changing Wage Type	48
45	Changing Withholding Allowances	49
46	Finding the Number of Employees in Each Department	49
47	Changing Addresses	50
48	Test—Quantum Corporation, Employee File	50

QUANTUM CORPORATION CLIENT FILE

Exercise	Title	Page
	Unit III – Quantum Corporation Client File	65
49A	Indexing Business and Organization Names	67
49B	Indexing Business and Organization Names With Punctuation	69
50A	Indexing Business and Organization Names With Numbers	71
50B	Indexing Government Names	73
50C	Optional Indexing Exercise—Indexing Client Names, Forms 001 Through 056	75
51	Creating the Client File	76
52	Creating a Customer Screen	77
53	Inputting Data From Forms 001 Through 024	77
54	Inputting Data From Forms 025 Through 056	78
55	Listing the Entire Client Field	78
56	Answering Client Inquiries	79
57	Finding the Number of Clients by Organization Type	81
58	Adding New Clients	81
59	Updating Client Records	82
60	Preparing Mailing Labels for Wholesalers	82
61	Finding the Researchers	82
62	Searching for Product-Service Categories	83
63	Searching for Clients in Los Angeles and Their Client Representatives	83
64	Reporting the Total Number of Clients Served by Each Client Representative	84
65	Deleting Client Records	84
66	Listing Washington State Retailers	84

Exercise	Title	Page

QUANTUM CORPORATION CLIENT FILE Continued

67	Listing the San Francisco Clients	85
68	Listing the Government Agencies	85
69	Updating Client Records	86
70	Adding More New Clients	86
71	Creating Mailing Labels for Selected Clients	86
72	Listing the Service Businesses in California	87
73	Preparing for Small-Organization Survey	87
74	Finding the Companies	88
75A	Test—Quantum Corporation, Client File	88
75B	Optional Exercises in Indexing and Data Entry	88

QUANTUM CORPORATION INVENTORY FILE

	Unit IV – Quantum Corporation Inventory File	**115**
76	Creating the File	117
77	Entering the Data	118
78	Listing the Records in the Database	119
79	Writing a Program/Macro	119
80	Searching for Service Vendors	120
81	Adding Records	121
82	Printing Computer Equipment in Report Form	122
83	Finding Equipment Needing Service	122
84	Searching for Expiration Dates	123
85	Helping the Office Manager	124
86	Updating Records	124
87	Altering the Database	125
88	Deleting Records	126
89	Finding Equipment Value	126
90	Answering Inquiries	127
91	Adding Records	128
92	Helping the Accountant	129
93	Changing a Service Vendor	129
94	Printing a Report to List Service Vendors	130
95	Revising an Expiration Date	130
96	Producing a Graph or Summary Record	131
97	Relating Equipment to Employees of Quantum	131
98	Preparing a Vendor Report	132
99	Answering Inquiries	132
100	Creating a Formal Printout	133
101	Test—Quantum Corporation's Inventory File	133

	Quantum Corporation Equipment Inventory List	135
	Tutorial	137
	Appendix	149

ABOUT THE AUTHORS

Jeffrey Stewart is Professor of Business Education and Program Area Leader at Virginia Polytechnic Institute and State University, Blacksburg, Virginia. He teaches both undergraduate and graduate courses in microcomputer applications for business. A widely published author, Dr. Stewart has written numerous books, workbooks, and practice sets in filing, records management, recordkeeping, and office procedures. He is a member of the Association of Records Managers and Administrators.

Sandra McMinnis teaches in the information systems program in the School of Business Administration, The Pennsylvania State University, Capital Campus, Harrisburg. Her background includes several years of teaching business and microcomputer applications at the high school, junior college, and university levels. She has conducted numerous seminars for major companies in both Virginia and Pennsylvania.

Nancy Melesco is a senior computer programmer analyst for Comdial Corporation, Charlottesville, Virginia. She designs and writes software for manufacturing and accounting applications. She is also a part-time instructor in computer science at Piedmont Virginia Community College.

The authors acknowledge David Adams, a senior at The Pennsylvania State University at Harrisburg and Janice Agee, business teacher at Arnold R. Burton Technology Center in Salem, Virginia, for their assistance in field testing portions of this text.

Introduction

The 101 exercises in this book will provide you with an opportunity to create four database files as you would in a real-life situation. In addition, you will learn how to index the names of individuals, businesses, organizations, and government agencies. Indexing these names will place them in computer files according to standard indexing rules developed by the Association of Records Managers and Administrators (ARMA). These exercises were developed to introduce you to electronic filing and to acquaint you with the new ARMA alphabetic indexing rules.

In completing the four units of the text-workbook, you will create and work with a customer file for Faunteroi's Department Store. In addition, you will work with (or) manage an employee file, a client file, and an equipment inventory file for Quantum Corporation.

After completing the exercises in this text-workbook, you will be able to do the following:

1. Enter names in indexed form into a computer file after you have been given the standard or letterhead form of a name (person, business, organization, or government agency).

2. Create a computer file and enter records into it.

3. Add new records to, and delete records from, a computer file.

4. Locate existing records in a computer file and update them.

5. Extract information from selected records in a computer file.

6. Print listings from a computer file in a specified order.

7. Print reports from a computer file which contain headings, rulings, counts, and totals.

8. Establish a relationship between two files that contain related data.

9. Extract information from more than one related file.

Overview– Working With a Database

In your business studies, you may have worked with database "files." Files may be papers stored in a file cabinet, a desk drawer, or a card file. However, all files do not have to be on paper. In this book, you will learn how to work with files that are stored electronically in computers rather than on paper. A group of computer files is called a database.

Computer databases enable you to keep large numbers of records on file that can be retrieved in a moment's notice. This capability is one of many that make database programs valuable to the business world.

Computer databases have several advantages over paper files. Some of these are: speed of finding records, ability to rearrange them very rapidly, and ability to store many of them in a small space.

The Units in this Book

This book contains four units. In each unit, you will set up a database file and maintain it. The units have been designed to be used with any type of database program. This also means that you can use any type of computer. Because of the popularity of two database programs, dBASE and Lotus, tutorials for doing the exercises with those programs are given on pages 000-000 of this book. The tutorials are detailed for the exercises in Unit I and become less specific in Units II, III, and IV.

Because these four units contain 101 exercises that may be used with any database program, you will need to study your database program manual before you begin the exercises. Your instructor will tell you which, if any, exercises cannot be completed with your database program.

In Unit I, you will work with a file of the customers of Faunteroi's Department Store. In Unit II, you will design and maintain a file of the employees of Quantum Corporation, a research firm. In Unit III, you will establish and maintain a file of the clients of Quantum Corporation. In both Unit I and Unit III, you will learn to enter names into a database in what is called indexed form. Unit IV provides data and exercises to set up an inventory file of the office equipment owned by Quantum.

Entering Names Into a Database

Databases are frequently established for customers, vendors, students, and other groups who need to use the names of individuals and organizations. Such information is usually entered into a file so that it can be sorted alphabetically. Computers will sort the names of individuals and organizations for us. However, there must be a procedure for arranging names in sequence. For this reason, the Association of Records Managers and Administrators (ARMA) has developed a set of standard rules for indexing and alphabetizing names.

Whenever you print an alphabetic list of the records in your database, you can expect to find any record quickly because it is in alphabetic order. It is important that you use the standard indexing rules in putting the names into the database so that they will be arranged in an easily retrievable manner.

How a Database is Organized

A field is a group of characters (letters, numbers, special characters, or spaces) that make up an item of information. In a relational database and most spreadsheet databases, the term field is also known as a column. Information is entered into a database one field at a time. A database might have fields for the social security number, name, ZIP code, and phone number of an individual. With some database programs, you must identify what type of field you will be using—character or numeric. Character fields, also called alphanumeric, are those that are made up of any combination of letters, numbers, or special characters. A field identified as a character field cannot be used for mathematical calculations. Names and addresses are examples of character fields. Numeric fields are made up of numbers only. They may also include a decimal point or a minus sign if the number is negative. Data is usually designated as numeric when it represents a value, such as an amount of money, and mathematical calculations are to be made using the field data. Remember, numbers such as your social security number or your phone number would be designated as character fields because they are not used for calculations and they normally include hyphens.

Groups of related fields make up a record. In a relational database and most spreadsheet databases, the term record is also known as a row. A record contains all the information about an individual or item. In Unit I, for example, each record contains information about one customer. In Unit IV, each record contains information about one item of office equipment. Each record will have at least one key field. A key field contains data that is unique to each record. This field is used to look up information in the file. For example, employees may be looked up by social security number or customers may be looked up by account number.

A file is made up of groups of related records. The term table is also used to describe related records in a database. In Unit III, you will work with an employee file made up of one record for each employee who works for Quantum Corporation.

A database is a collection of related files. The employee file in Unit II, the client file in Unit III, and the inventory file in Unit IV are three parts of Quantum Corporation's database. By linking files into a database, a company can combine information from several different files to handle complex management needs. The relationships between a field (column), a record (row), a file (table), and a database are illustrated below.

230-11-6670	FIELD (COLUMN)

230-11-6670	GREEN	CHARLES	S	SALESPERSON	11.35	RECORD (ROW)

230-16-6011	WEBB	ESTELLA	A	SALESPERSON	12.35
226-14-6679	PEREZ	CARLOS	A	SUPERVISOR	15.52
223-88-2311	LYLE	GEORGE	E	LINE WORKER	11.15
230-11-6670	GREEN	CHARLES	S	SALESPERSON	11.35

FILE (TABLE)

DATABASE

TY13	ELECTRONIC TYPEWRITER	60009988E	750.00
EM11	DATA ENTRY MACHINE	D00066943	1980.00
CP20	COMPUTER TERMINAL	T7778436	1200.00
AM11	ANSWERING MACHINE	97A0109	295.00

FILE (TABLE)

FAUNTEROI'S CUSTOMER FILE

Faunteroi's is a department store with headquarters in Louisville, Kentucky. Growth over the past few years has brought new branch stores to Indiana and Ohio. Faunteroi's accepts cash, major credit cards, and its own Faunteroi card. It considers its customers who have a Faunteroi card to be special. These customers often receive mailings notifying them of sales and other privileges before they are advertised to the public. Sometimes, Faunteroi cardholders are given discount coupons which are not offered to others. The managers of Faunteroi's believe that issuing the Faunteroi card helps to increase sales, but they contend with the usual problems of collecting debts and keeping customer credit ratings up-to-date.

The president of Faunteroi's has decided to change the company's recordkeeping operations. With the store's rapid expansion and growth in sales, the old method has become too slow and expensive.

Company management wants you to develop a computer file of its customer records. It will also be your job to maintain this file. It will be used to organize customer mailings announcing special sales, to answer inquiries from the accounts receivable department about customer accounts, and to perform a variety of other tasks. You will use the file to respond to these requests quickly and accurately.

Before you can create the file of customers, you must learn two methods of entering their names into the file for computer use. Names of individuals may be written in two ways:

1. In *standard* form, or the way you might sign your name—for example: Carmen L. Sanchez. In standard form, the first name is first, followed by the middle initial or name, and the last name. Names are sometimes entered into computer files in standard form so the names can later be printed on correspondence, envelope labels, and other forms on which you want the first name to appear first, followed by the middle initial or name, and last name. The entire name may be entered into the computer as one field, or each part of the name (first name, middle initial or name, and last name) may be entered into a separate field. In this unit, the standard form name is entered as one field.

2. In *indexed* form, or the way your name might appear in a phone book—for example: SANCHEZ CARMEN L. Notice that the indexed form is written in all capitals and that the period after the initial is omitted. An indexed name of an individual is arranged by last name, first name, and then middle initial or name. In this unit, you will enter the indexed name as one field.

Faunteroi's wishes to enter customer names in both standard and indexed form for the following reasons:

1. Having the names in standard form will enable Faunteroi's to print them on correspondence, labels, and other forms with the first name first, followed by the middle name or initial, and last name.

2. Having the name in indexed form will enable Faunteroi's to arrange the records in alphabetic order by each customer's last name.

The input forms on pages 00-00 contain customers' names in standard form. They also contain spaces for you to enter the name in indexed form. Exercises 1A, 1B, and 2A and 2B provide practice in indexing individual names using the rules compatible with those of the Association of Records Managers and Administrators (ARMA).

EXERCISE 1A

Indexing Names of Individuals

Name _____ Date _____

Section _____ Evaluation _____

STUDY THE INDEXING RULE

Each part of a name is considered to be a *unit*. For example, *Thomas Alan Nelson* contains three units. To index the name, list the units in the order shown below. Remember to leave a space between each unit.

First: surname (last name)

Second: given name (first name) or initial

Third: middle initial or name

This means that you can transpose (or switch) the last name to be the first unit, as shown in these examples.

Note: The indexed form is in capital letters.

STANDARD FORM	INDEXED FORM
Cecil D. Aaron	AARON CECIL D
Daniel James Abel	ABEL DANIEL JAMES
T. Cary Abel	ABEL T CARY
S. Thomas Apple	APPLE S THOMAS
Susan Ann Apple	APPLE SUSAN ANN
Charles Perry Appleton	APPLETON CHARLES PERRY

Note that the above names are arranged in alphabetic order and that *S. Thomas Apple* comes before *Susan Ann Apple*. This is because of a rule that states "Nothing comes before something." Why do you think *Susan Ann Apple* is listed before *Charles Perry Appleton*?

PRACTICE INDEXING

Write each name in indexed form as shown in the example. Remember, when indexing, use all capital letters. Be sure to omit the period after each initial.

0. Paula E. French

   |F|R|E|N|C|H| |P|A|U|L|A| |E| | | | | | | | | | | | | | | |

1. Henry J. Garfield

   | | | | | | | | | | | | | | | | | | | | | | | | | | | | | | | | |

2. T. Walker Garst

   | | | | | | | | | | | | | | | | | | | | | | | | | | | | | | | | |

3.   Mary Ann Glidden

|└┴┴┴┴┴┴┴┴┴┴┴┴┴┴┴┴┴┴┴┴┴┴┴┴┴┴┴┴┴┴┴┴┘|

4.   Teresa M. Glowinski

|└┴┴┴┴┴┴┴┴┴┴┴┴┴┴┴┴┴┴┴┴┴┴┴┴┴┴┴┴┴┴┴┴┘|

5.   O. T. Hall

|└┴┴┴┴┴┴┴┴┴┴┴┴┴┴┴┴┴┴┴┴┴┴┴┴┴┴┴┴┴┴┴┴┘|

6.   Cecil M. Mattox

|└┴┴┴┴┴┴┴┴┴┴┴┴┴┴┴┴┴┴┴┴┴┴┴┴┴┴┴┴┴┴┴┴┘|

EXERCISE 1B

Indexing Personal Names With Prefixes

Name _____   Date _____

Section _____   Evaluation _____

STUDY THE INDEXING RULE

Some names have a prefix. The *Mc* in *McDonald* is a surname prefix. A prefix should be considered as a part of the name rather than as a separate unit. In order to be sure that the computer will sort prefixes properly, enter names with prefixes into the computer without spaces or punctuation. Common prefixes include: *d', D', Da, de, De, de la, Del, Des, Di, Du, El, Fitz, La, Le, Les, M', Mac, Mc, O', St., Ste., Saint, Van, Van de, Van der, Von, and Von der*. The name *de Leon* is indexed *DELEON*, without the space. How do you index *Mac Allister*?

Note these other examples.

STANDARD FORM	INDEXED FORM
Pana El Greco	ELGRECO PANA
Suzanne M. LaFevre	LAFEVRE SUZANNE M
William O. McConnel	MCCONNEL WILLIAM O
P. Shawn O'Dell	ODELL P SHAWN
Caroll D. St. James	STJAMES CAROLL D
Frederick K. Von Neuman	VONNEUMAN FREDERICK K

PRACTICE INDEXING

Write each name in indexed form as shown in the example.

0. Ann M. d'Arcy

   |D|A|R|C|Y| |A|N|N| |M| | | | | | | | | | | | | |C| | |

1. Marion E. de la France

2. Vickie Rae de Luce

3. Samuel William DuPont

4. Dorothy C. FitzPatrick

5

5. N. Marcia MacGregor

    |_|_|_|_|_|_|_|_|_|_|_|_|_|_|_|_|_|_|_|_|_|_|_|_|_|_|_|_|_|_|_|_|_|_|_|_|_|_|_|

6. Sara Ellen Mack

    |_|_|_|_|_|_|_|_|_|_|_|_|_|_|_|_|_|_|_|_|_|_|_|_|_|_|_|_|_|_|_|_|_|_|_|_|_|_|_|

7. Erin O'Hara

    |_|_|_|_|_|_|_|_|_|_|_|_|_|_|_|_|_|_|_|_|_|_|_|_|_|_|_|_|_|_|_|_|_|_|_|_|_|_|_|

8. Paul Simon Ste. Marie

    |_|_|_|_|_|_|_|_|_|_|_|_|_|_|_|_|_|_|_|_|_|_|_|_|_|_|_|_|_|_|_|_|_|_|_|_|_|_|_|

9. Robert C. van der Pelt

    |_|_|_|_|_|_|_|_|_|_|_|_|_|_|_|_|_|_|_|_|_|_|_|_|_|_|_|_|_|_|_|_|_|_|_|_|_|_|_|

10. Peter T. Van Heussen

    |_|_|_|_|_|_|_|_|_|_|_|_|_|_|_|_|_|_|_|_|_|_|_|_|_|_|_|_|_|_|_|_|_|_|_|_|_|_|_|

EXERCISE 2A

Indexing Names With Titles and Suffixes

Name _____   Date _____

Section _____   Evaluation _____

STUDY THE INDEXING RULE

Prefixes, such as professional titles (Dr., Mayor, Capt., and Senator), and suffixes, such as seniority terms (Sr., Jr., and 3d), or professional degrees (C.P.A., Ph.D., and M.D.) are used as units to distinguish between otherwise identical names. The prefix or suffix is the last unit.

STANDARD FORM	INDEXED FORM
Samuel B. Mason, 3d	MASON SAMUEL B 3D
Samuel B. Mason, C.P.A.	MASON SAMUEL B CPA
Dr. Samuel B. Mason	MASON SAMUEL B DR
Lt. Samuel B. Mason	MASON SAMUEL B LT
Lt. Sandra B. Mason	MASON SANDRA B LT

PRACTICE INDEXING

Write each name in indexed form as shown in the examples.

0. B. Joseph Banes

    |B|A|N|E|S| |B| |J|O|S|E|P|H| | | | | | | | | | | | | | | |

1. B. Joseph Banes, 2d

    |B|A|N|E|S| |B| |J|O|S|E|P|H| |2|D| | | | | | | | | | | |

2. Stella L. Fraser

    | | | | | | | | | | | | | | | | | | | | | | | | | | | | | | | |

3. Maj. Stella L. Fraser

    | | | | | | | | | | | | | | | | | | | | | | | | | | | | | | | |

4. Harold C. Hall

    | | | | | | | | | | | | | | | | | | | | | | | | | | | | | | | |

5. Harold C. Hall, 3d

    | | | | | | | | | | | | | | | | | | | | | | | | | | | | | | | |

6. Harold C. Hall, 4th

   |_|_|_|_|_|_|_|_|_|_|_|_|_|_|_|_|_|_|_|_|_|_|_|_|_|_|_|_|_|_|_|_|_|_|_|_|_|_|_|_|_|_|_|_|_|

7. Harold C. Hall, D.D.S.

   |_|_|_|_|_|_|_|_|_|_|_|_|_|_|_|_|_|_|_|_|_|_|_|_|_|_|_|_|_|_|_|_|_|_|_|_|_|_|_|_|_|_|_|_|_|

8. Maj. Harold C. Hall

   |_|_|_|_|_|_|_|_|_|_|_|_|_|_|_|_|_|_|_|_|_|_|_|_|_|_|_|_|_|_|_|_|_|_|_|_|_|_|_|_|_|_|_|_|_|

9. Senator Harold C. Hall

   |_|_|_|_|_|_|_|_|_|_|_|_|_|_|_|_|_|_|_|_|_|_|_|_|_|_|_|_|_|_|_|_|_|_|_|_|_|_|_|_|_|_|_|_|_|

10. Harold C. Hall, Sr.

   |_|_|_|_|_|_|_|_|_|_|_|_|_|_|_|_|_|_|_|_|_|_|_|_|_|_|_|_|_|_|_|_|_|_|_|_|_|_|_|_|_|_|_|_|_|

EXERCISE 2B

Indexing Hyphenated Personal Names

PAUNTLAUN
CUSTOMER FILE

Name _____ Date _____

Section _____ Evaluation _____

STUDY THE INDEXING RULE

When a person has a hyphenated first or last name, ignore the hyphen and enter the name as one indexing unit.

STANDARD FORM	**INDEXED FORM**
Dee-Dee Ashton	ASHTON DEEDEE
Martin R. Fitz-Simmons	FITZSIMMONS MARTIN R
Jo-anne B. Mayo	MAYO JOANNE B
Mary Jo Parker-Adams	PARKERADAMS MARY JO

PRACTICE INDEXING

Write each name in indexed form as shown in the example.

0.   Jo-Lynn Claire-Adams

   |C|L|A|I|R|E|A|D|A|M|S| |J|O|L|Y|N|N| | | | | | | | |

1.   Jeanne-Marie LaFrance

   | | | | | | | | | | | | | | | | | | | | | | | | | | | | | | | | | |

2.   Tony L. Saint-Paul

   | | | | | | | | | | | | | | | | | | | | | | | | | | | | | | | | | |

3.   Suzie Ta-Lien

   | | | | | | | | | | | | | | | | | | | | | | | | | | | | | | | | | |

4.   Anna-Marie Louise Vincent

   | | | | | | | | | | | | | | | | | | | | | | | | | | | | | | | | | |

Optional Indexing Exercise — Indexing Customer Names, Forms 001 Through 036

Name _____   Date _____

Section _____   Evaluation _____

Faunteroi's   CUSTOMER ACCOUNT FORM   001

__ NEW   __ CHANGE   __ DELETE

ACCOUNT |NAME
NUMBER |
                 |

INDEXED
NAME
    | | | | | | | | | | | | | | | | | | | | | | | | | | | | | | | | |

ADDRESS |CITY |STATE |ZIP
                           | | |

CREDIT |CREDIT |BALANCE |
RATING |LIMIT |DUE |
            | | |

Information about Faunteroi's customers has been kept on forms such as the one illustrated here. There are four forms to a page.

In this optional exercise, you will prepare the forms to be used as source documents for entering the data into the computer file. Follow these steps:

1.   Turn to page 23 and find Faunteroi's customer account form number 001. The form numbers are in the upper-right corner and are only for reference in this book.

2.   Note that the name of the customer is *Douglas J. Hill*. The name is written in standard form.

3.   Note that there are blank spaces for the indexed name. Write the indexed form in all capital letters in the spaces. Write one letter in each space. Leave a space between units. The Indexed Name section of form 001 should look like this.

INDEXED
NAME |H|I|L|L| |D|O|U|G|L|A|S| |J| | | | | | | | | | | | |

4.   Follow Step 3 for forms 002 through 036. Your instructor may have you check your work against the key on page 149 and make corrections if necessary.

EXERCISE

3

Creating the File

Name _____ Date _____

Section _____ Evaluation _____

Note: Your instructor may tell you to skip this exercise if you are using the data diskette.

In this exercise you will create a computer file containing the data shown on customer account forms 001 through 036. Be sure that you know how to use your computer and your database program before you begin. With some programs, you can design data entry screens to look like the source document. With others, you enter each field name on a line and specify the length and type of field.

Hint: With some databases it is a good idea to type your field names in all caps. Note the example below:

FIELD NAME → NAME: Margaret E. Chambers ← *DATA*

FIELD NAME → CITY: Louisville   ← *DATA*

This makes it easy to tell the field name from the data when you proofread your entries and get information from your file.

For some database programs, you must know the *field length,* or the exact number of characters in each field. You might also have to tell whether the field is character or numeric. If you are using a spreadsheet database, you will also have to adjust column widths to accommodate both the data and the column heading. Field information for the Faunteroi's customer file is below:

FIELD CONTENTS	FIELD NAME	FIELD LENGTH	TYPE
Account Number	ACCOUNT_NO	5	CHARACTER
Name	NAME	28	CHARACTER
Indexed Name	INDEX_NAME	28	CHARACTER
Address	ADDRESS	25	CHARACTER
City	CITY	20	CHARACTER
State	STATE	2	CHARACTER
ZIP Code	ZIP	5	CHARACTER
Credit Rating	CREDIT_RAT	1	NUMERIC
Credit Limit	CREDIT_LMT	4	NUMERIC
Balance Due	BALANCEDUE	7	NUMERIC

EXERCISE 4

Keying Data From Forms 001 Through 036

Name _____ Date _____

Section _____ Evaluation _____

Note: Your instructor may tell you to skip this exercise if you are using the data diskette.

In this exercise, you will enter the data from the customer account forms into the database. Remove forms 001 through 036, pages 23 through 31. Remember, key the data from each form field by field. Save forms 037 through 040 for Exercise 9.

After you complete the entries for each form, be sure to check your work. By correcting any errors before processing the next form, you will save yourself a great deal of trouble later.

EXERCISE 5

Listing Customer Names and Account Numbers

Name _____ Date _____

Section _____ Evaluation _____

A *listing* is simply a hard copy of how data are stored in a database. A listing appears in the same format as that used when the items were keyed.

A *report printout* shows the data in a certain format. Usually there are report headings, column headings, page numbers, and other features such as centered titles. A report printout is similar to a typewritten report.

Most companies want a listing of all records in their files. It serves as an extra backup and a way to find information in the file when a computer is not handy. Usually, the entire file is printed out. Sometimes only the affected records are printed when an addition or an update is made to the file. In the exercises in this book, you do not need to reprint the entire file after you make each addition, deletion, or change.

In this exercise, you are to print a list of all customers. Include the Account Number and Name fields only. Review your database software manual for information on how to print from a file. Your listing should be in alphabetic order.

Note: Be sure to use the Indexed Name field when sorting. Do not use the Name field.

With some database systems, the default option is to print one customer account form per page. If your database operates this way you must change the default setting or you will use 36 sheets of paper. To do this, figure the number of lines of print each form will take. You can print as many as 66 lines on a standard 8 1/2- X 11-inch sheet of paper. Divide the number of lines each form will take into 66 to find the number of forms you can print per page. For example, if each form takes 10 lines to print, divide 10 into 66. Round down the answer, 6.6, to the nearest whole number, 6. This means that you will have six forms printed on each page instead of only one.

EXERCISE 6

Proofreading Your Listing

Name _____ Date _____

Section _____ Evaluation _____

After you have completed your listing, proofread it carefully for errors. Even though you have checked the information on each screen, you must take the time now to recheck the keyed data. Any errors will affect the information you obtain from your file. If you find any errors, make the corrections now. Turn to page 149 to check your work against the key to make sure that your list is in proper alphabetic order by indexed name.

EXERCISE

7

Helping the Accountant

Name _____ Date _____

Section _____ Evaluation _____

Use the Faunteroi's customer file to do the following work. Write your answers in the spaces provided.

One of the store's accountants sent you a memo asking for the following information:

a. The account numbers of all customers living in Louisville, KY.

_____ _____ _____ _____

_____ _____ _____ _____

_____ _____ _____ _____

_____ _____ _____ _____

_____

b. The account numbers of all customers whose balance due is more than $2000.

_____ _____ _____

c. The account numbers of all customers whose credit rating is *3* and whose balance due is greater than $500. Faunteroi's uses the following codes to indicate a customer's credit rating:

1— Good credit rating

2— Fair credit rating

3— Poor credit rating

_____ _____

d. How many customers live in Ohio? _____

How many live in Indiana? _____

How many live in Kentucky? _____

EXERCISE
8
Finding the Customers

Name _____   Date _____

Section _____   Evaluation _____

The manager of the customer relations department wants to know how many customers do not live in the states in which a Faunteroi's store is located—that is, those who do not live in Kentucky (KY), Ohio (OH), and Indiana (IN). How many? _____

EXERCISE
9
Adding New Customers

Name _____   Date _____

Section _____   Evaluation _____

Faunteroi's is always happy to acquire new credit card customers. The credit manager has sent you the customer account forms for four new customers and has asked you to add them to the database files. Using forms 037 through 040, write the indexed form of each name. Now add these new customers to the file. Note at the top of each form that the "New" box has been checked.

EXERCISE
10
Updating Records

Name _____   Date _____

Section _____   Evaluation _____

From time to time it is necessary to update or change some customer records. The customer relations and credit departments have submitted several changes. Turn to page 33 and remove forms 041 through 044. (Be sure to keep forms 045 through 048 for Exercise 14.) Note that the "Change" box has been checked on these four forms. Note also that the forms are not completely filled out. When a change is made in a customer account record, only the account number or customer name and the specific change are recorded on the form. Make the changes to these customer records.

EXERCISE 11

Printing Mailing Labels

Name _____ Date _____

Section _____ Evaluation _____

The advertising department has a special promotional mailing that must be sent to customers in Louisville. Select these customers and print mailing labels for them. Sort the labels by ZIP code so that postage can be saved.

EXERCISE 12

Printing a Customer Report

Name _____ Date _____

Section _____ Evaluation _____

The credit manager wants a report sorted by account number of all customers whose balance due is more than $1000. Include the following fields in your report and provide in it a count of the number of listed customers.

Account Number

Name

Credit Rating

Credit Limit

Balance Due

EXERCISE 13

Answering Phone Inquiries

Name _____ Date _____

Section _____ Evaluation _____

a. The credit manager's secretary called to request the credit rating for Mr. Hallstrum (Halstead? or Halstom?). _____

b. An assistant in the credit department wants the balance due for Roberto Manuel.

_____

c. A salesperson asks for an approval to grant credit to Joel Allen for $159. (Find his record, add $159 to his balance due, and if the total is less than his credit limit, it is all right to grant credit.)

Approved _____ Not Approved _____

d. The credit manager wants the account number of Sandra St. James and the address of James Fuller. Find this information:

Sandra St. James' account number is _____

James Fuller's address is _____

EXERCISE 14

Deleting Records

Name _____ Date _____

Section _____ Evaluation _____

Faunteroi's sometimes has customers who have not used their credit cards for a long time or who should be removed from the files for various reasons. You have been sent customer account forms for several inactive accounts that are to be deleted from the file. Remove forms 045 through 048 and delete the appropriate records.

Note: The "Delete" box has been checked on each form and only the account number has been filled in.

17

15

Listing Paid - Up Customers

Name _____   Date _____

Section _____   Evaluation _____

Prepare an alphabetized list of names and account numbers of any customers in the file who have a zero (0) balance due. You may print the Indexed Name field or the Name field along with the account number. The credit manager wants to check to see whether these accounts are still active.

16

Checking Credit Limits

Name _____   Date _____

Section _____   Evaluation _____

Print a list of customers with a credit limit of $500 and a credit rating of *1*. Faunteroi's might want to increase the credit limit for these customers. Include Account Number, Name, and Balance Due fields in your report. Before printing the report, sort your file in alphabetic order by indexed name.

EXERCISE 17

Modifying the Database Structure and Updating Records

Name _____ Date _____

Section _____ Evaluation _____

a. Management has decided to provide for nine-digit ZIP codes. Nine-digit ZIP codes require a field length of 10 because there is a hyphen after the first five digits: 23124-1200. Because there is a hyphen and no calculations are to be made, this is a character field. Change your database structure so the ZIP code field has a length of 10 characters.

b. Additional records are to be updated. Remove forms 049 through 052, page 35, and key the changes. Keep forms 053 through 056 for Exercise 18.

EXERCISE 18

Adding More New Customers

Name _____ Date _____

Section _____ Evaluation _____

Once again Faunteroi's has new customers to be added to the data file. Remove forms 053 through 056 to index the names and add the records.

19

19 Answering More Inquiries

Name _____ Date _____

Section _____ Evaluation _____

a. A sales associate requests approval to grant credit for $450 to account number 23244.

Approved _____ Not Approved _____

b. The credit manager wants the following information for M. S. Bezzini:

Balance Due: _____

Credit Rating: _____

Credit Limit: _____

c. A sales associate asks for an approval to grant credit to Jeron P. Saunders for $150. (The associate, Jodi Wells, says she is not certain about the spelling of this customer's last name.)

Approved _____ Not Approved _____

d. The credit manager requests Patrick Grogan's address.

_____

_____

e. The credit manager asks for information about Lt. Allen:

Credit Rating: _____

Credit Limit: _____

Balance Due: _____

20

EXERCISE
20

Reporting Preferred Customers

Name _____   Date _____

Section _____   Evaluation _____

Print a report containing the name (use the Name field) and address for all customers who have a credit limit of $5000. Faunteroi's wishes to offer them a preferred-customer special. Sort the report by city because all customers in one city will be contacted at once. Provide a count of customers.

EXERCISE
21

Test – Faunteroi's

Your instructor will give you the test for this unit.

Faunteroi's

[X] NEW   [ ] CHANGE   [ ] DELETE

| ACCOUNT NUMBER | 10934 | NAME | Douglas J. Hill |

INDEXED NAME

ADDRESS	CITY	STATE	ZIP
245 1st Street NE	Louisville	KY	40243

| CREDIT RATING | 2 | CREDIT LIMIT | 500 | BALANCE DUE | 100 |

Faunteroi's

CUSTOMER ACCOUNT FORM 002

[X] NEW   [ ] CHANGE   [ ] DELETE

| ACCOUNT NUMBER | 19357 | NAME | William Edward Shelton |

INDEXED NAME

ADDRESS	CITY	STATE	ZIP
2425 Wood Lake Terrace	Louisville	KY	40222

| CREDIT RATING | 1 | CREDIT LIMIT | 5000 | BALANCE DUE | 0 |

Faunteroi's

CUSTOMER ACCOUNT FORM 003

[X] NEW   [ ] CHANGE   [ ] DELETE

| ACCOUNT NUMBER | 20109 | NAME | Colleen T. Van Horn |

INDEXED NAME

ADDRESS	CITY	STATE	ZIP
2708 Fox Hunt Drive	Louisville	KY	40287

| CREDIT RATING | 1 | CREDIT LIMIT | 5000 | BALANCE DUE | 92.58 |

Faunteroi's

CUSTOMER ACCOUNT FORM 004

[X] NEW   [ ] CHANGE   [ ] DELETE

| ACCOUNT NUMBER | 20304 | NAME | Joseph J. Zimmerman |

INDEXED NAME

ADDRESS	CITY	STATE	ZIP
457 St. James Street	Reily	OH	45056

| CREDIT RATING | 1 | CREDIT LIMIT | 1000 | BALANCE DUE | 0 |

Faunteroi's

[X] NEW   [ ] CHANGE   [ ] DELETE

ACCOUNT NUMBER	23244	NAME	Faleh Mohammed Al-Shammari

INDEXED NAME

ADDRESS	CITY	STATE	ZIP
4526 Lauren Circle	Louisville	KY	40222

CREDIT RATING	1	CREDIT LIMIT	5000	BALANCE DUE	359.99

Faunteroi's

[X] NEW   [ ] CHANGE   [ ] DELETE

ACCOUNT NUMBER	24083	NAME	Steven M. Greensfelt

INDEXED NAME

ADDRESS	CITY	STATE	ZIP
2458 Barca Drive	Cincinnati	OH	45207

CREDIT RATING	1	CREDIT LIMIT	5000	BALANCE DUE	1200.00

Faunteroi's

[X] NEW   [ ] CHANGE   [ ] DELETE

ACCOUNT NUMBER	26261	NAME	Lt. Joel P. Allen

INDEXED NAME

ADDRESS	CITY	STATE	ZIP
2426 Colonial Drive	Modesto	CA	95350

CREDIT RATING	2	CREDIT LIMIT	500	BALANCE DUE	400.00

Faunteroi's

[X] NEW   [ ] CHANGE   [ ] DELETE

ACCOUNT NUMBER	29034	NAME	Paul Lynn Wright

INDEXED NAME

ADDRESS	CITY	STATE	ZIP
231 G Street	Louisville	KY	40220

CREDIT RATING	2	CREDIT LIMIT	500	BALANCE DUE	159.00

Faunteroi's

[X] NEW　　　[ ] CHANGE　　　[ ] DELETE

ACCOUNT NUMBER	29265	NAME	Jennifer Lynn L'Abbie

INDEXED NAME																									

ADDRESS	CITY	STATE	ZIP
7545 Moccasin Trail	Louisville	KY	40210

CREDIT RATING	2	CREDIT LIMIT	500	BALANCE DUE	0

Faunteroi's

[X] NEW　　　[ ] CHANGE　　　[ ] DELETE

ACCOUNT NUMBER	30272	NAME	T. Dalton Taylor

INDEXED NAME																									

ADDRESS	CITY	STATE	ZIP
Rt. 6 Box 665	Aberdeen	OH	45101

CREDIT RATING	1	CREDIT LIMIT	500	BALANCE DUE	0

Faunteroi's

[X] NEW　　　[ ] CHANGE　　　[ ] DELETE

ACCOUNT NUMBER	34343	NAME	Martin G. McMichael

INDEXED NAME																									

ADDRESS	CITY	STATE	ZIP
Rt. 6 Box 6	Reily	OH	45056

CREDIT RATING	1	CREDIT LIMIT	5000	BALANCE DUE	207.67

Faunteroi's

[X] NEW　　　[ ] CHANGE　　　[ ] DELETE

ACCOUNT NUMBER	34923	NAME	Roberto F. Manuel

INDEXED NAME																									

ADDRESS	CITY	STATE	ZIP
189 Salazar Drive	Cincinnati	OH	45248

CREDIT RATING	3	CREDIT LIMIT	500	BALANCE DUE	109.00

Faunteroi's

CUSTOMER ACCOUNT FORM   **013**

☒ NEW   ☐ CHANGE   ☐ DELETE

ACCOUNT NUMBER	34929	NAME	George W. Smith

INDEXED NAME																							

ADDRESS	CITY	STATE	ZIP
544 L'Angostino Drive	Lake of the Forest	KS	66012

CREDIT RATING	2	CREDIT LIMIT	1000	BALANCE DUE	754.88

Faunteroi's

CUSTOMER ACCOUNT FORM   **014**

☒ NEW   ☐ CHANGE   ☐ DELETE

ACCOUNT NUMBER	34962	NAME	Peter M. Hancock

INDEXED NAME																							

ADDRESS	CITY	STATE	ZIP
R. R. 624	Bennington	IN	47011

CREDIT RATING	1	CREDIT LIMIT	5000	BALANCE DUE	154.99

Faunteroi's

CUSTOMER ACCOUNT FORM   **015**

☒ NEW   ☐ CHANGE   ☐ DELETE

ACCOUNT NUMBER	38391	NAME	Jeron P. Sanders

INDEXED NAME																							

ADDRESS	CITY	STATE	ZIP
33 Rockland Boulevard	Joplin	MO	64801

CREDIT RATING	1	CREDIT LIMIT	5000	BALANCE DUE	456.79

Faunteroi's

CUSTOMER ACCOUNT FORM   **016**

☒ NEW   ☐ CHANGE   ☐ DELETE

ACCOUNT NUMBER	38921	NAME	James P. Fuller

INDEXED NAME																							

ADDRESS	CITY	STATE	ZIP
890 South Main Street	Bennington	IN	47011

CREDIT RATING	3	CREDIT LIMIT	500	BALANCE DUE	0

Faunteroi's

CUSTOMER ACCOUNT FORM 017

[X] NEW [ ] CHANGE [ ] DELETE

ACCOUNT NUMBER	41010	NAME	Leon W. Popek

INDEXED NAME

ADDRESS	654 Clearwater Court	CITY	Columbus	STATE	IN	ZIP	47216

CREDIT RATING	1	CREDIT LIMIT	5000	BALANCE DUE	1400.00

Faunteroi's

CUSTOMER ACCOUNT FORM 018

[X] NEW [ ] CHANGE [ ] DELETE

ACCOUNT NUMBER	42902	NAME	Sarah L. Proske

INDEXED NAME

ADDRESS	254 Forest Hill Avenue	CITY	Louisville	STATE	KY	ZIP	40221

CREDIT RATING	1	CREDIT LIMIT	1000	BALANCE DUE	285.66

Faunteroi's

CUSTOMER ACCOUNT FORM 019

[X] NEW [ ] CHANGE [ ] DELETE

ACCOUNT NUMBER	43028	NAME	Chee Won Kim

INDEXED NAME

ADDRESS	254 North 25th Stteet	CITY	Dayton	STATE	OH	ZIP	45444

CREDIT RATING	1	CREDIT LIMIT	5000	BALANCE DUE	500.00

Faunteroi's

CUSTOMER ACCOUNT FORM 020

[X] NEW [ ] CHANGE [ ] DELETE

ACCOUNT NUMBER	47282	NAME	D. Sanders Shelley

INDEXED NAME

ADDRESS	786 Indian Ridge Road	CITY	Louisville	STATE	KY	ZIP	40299

CREDIT RATING	3	CREDIT LIMIT	1000	BALANCE DUE	567.86

Faunteroi's

[X] NEW ☐ CHANGE ☐ DELETE

ACCOUNT NUMBER	48320	NAME	Serena K. Roth-Barre

INDEXED NAME

ADDRESS	CITY	STATE	ZIP
252 Flower Creek Lane	Louisville	KY	40220

CREDIT RATING	1	CREDIT LIMIT	1000	BALANCE DUE	256.39

Faunteroi's

[X] NEW ☐ CHANGE ☐ DELETE

ACCOUNT NUMBER	49802	NAME	Sandra T. St. James

INDEXED NAME

ADDRESS	CITY	STATE	ZIP
78 La Cueva Drive	Columbus	IN	47202

CREDIT RATING	3	CREDIT LIMIT	500	BALANCE DUE	498.00

Faunteroi's

[X] NEW ☐ CHANGE ☐ DELETE

ACCOUNT NUMBER	52973	NAME	Cynthia C. Kimbell

INDEXED NAME

ADDRESS	CITY	STATE	ZIP
2525 South Delaney Street	Cincinnati	OH	45230

CREDIT RATING	2	CREDIT LIMIT	1000	BALANCE DUE	0

Faunteroi's

[X] NEW ☐ CHANGE ☐ DELETE

ACCOUNT NUMBER	54871	NAME	Amy Lewis Busch-Mattox

INDEXED NAME

ADDRESS	CITY	STATE	ZIP
85 Glouster Circle	Louisville	OH	40220

CREDIT RATING	1	CREDIT LIMIT	5000	BALANCE DUE	0

Faunteroi's

[X] NEW   [ ] CHANGE   [ ] DELETE

ACCOUNT NUMBER	NAME
56721	Mario S. Bezzini

INDEXED NAME

ADDRESS	CITY	STATE	ZIP
P.O. Box 2745	Bennington	IN	47011

CREDIT RATING	CREDIT LIMIT	BALANCE DUE
3	1000	842.39

Faunteroi's

CUSTOMER ACCOUNT FORM 026

[X] NEW   [ ] CHANGE   [ ] DELETE

ACCOUNT NUMBER	NAME
57392	Miguel Ricardo Edwardo Oritz

INDEXED NAME

ADDRESS	CITY	STATE	ZIP
2425 Las Marinas Avenue	Louisville	KY	40213

CREDIT RATING	CREDIT LIMIT	BALANCE DUE
1	5000	3030.30

Faunteroi's

CUSTOMER ACCOUNT FORM 027

[X] NEW   [ ] CHANGE   [ ] DELETE

ACCOUNT NUMBER	NAME
60432	Sumio Fujita

INDEXED NAME

ADDRESS	CITY	STATE	ZIP
26 Jasmine Court	Cincinnati	OH	45225

CREDIT RATING	CREDIT LIMIT	BALANCE DUE
1	500	124.99

Faunteroi's

CUSTOMER ACCOUNT FORM 028

[X] NEW   [ ] CHANGE   [ ] DELETE

ACCOUNT NUMBER	NAME
63632	Mercedes Joaquina Oritz

INDEXED NAME

ADDRESS	CITY	STATE	ZIP
656 Cabo Blanco Way	Cincinnati	OH	45225

CREDIT RATING	CREDIT LIMIT	BALANCE DUE
1	5000	200.20

Faunteroi's

[X] NEW   [ ] CHANGE   [ ] DELETE

ACCOUNT NUMBER	64656	NAME	Dr. Thomas T. Rozenthall

INDEXED NAME

ADDRESS	8525 Breezy Lane	CITY	Cincinnati	STATE	OH	ZIP	45226

CREDIT RATING	1	CREDIT LIMIT	5000	BALANCE DUE	79.85

Faunteroi's

[X] NEW   [ ] CHANGE   [ ] DELETE

ACCOUNT NUMBER	76405	NAME	R. K. Halstrom

INDEXED NAME

ADDRESS	368 Glenview Drive	CITY	Louisville	STATE	KY	ZIP	40225

CREDIT RATING	3	CREDIT LIMIT	500	BALANCE DUE	498.00

Faunteroi's

[X] NEW   [ ] CHANGE   [ ] DELETE

ACCOUNT NUMBER	83929	NAME	Juanita Carmen Casquez

INDEXED NAME

ADDRESS	35 Rio Seco Drive	CITY	Cincinnati	STATE	OH	ZIP	45210

CREDIT RATING	3	CREDIT LIMIT	1000	BALANCE DUE	0

Faunteroi's

[X] NEW   [ ] CHANGE   [ ] DELETE

ACCOUNT NUMBER	84753	NAME	Adolfo Carrera

INDEXED NAME

ADDRESS	920 San Fidel Avenue	CITY	Louisville	STATE	KY	ZIP	40210

CREDIT RATING	3	CREDIT LIMIT	500	BALANCE DUE	0

Faunteroi's

[X] NEW [ ] CHANGE [ ] DELETE

ACCOUNT NUMBER	89824	NAME	G. Washington Smith

INDEXED NAME

ADDRESS	CITY	STATE	ZIP
224 Breezy Lane	Dayton	OH	45437

CREDIT RATING	3	CREDIT LIMIT	500	BALANCE DUE	125.00

Faunteroi's

[X] NEW [ ] CHANGE [ ] DELETE

ACCOUNT NUMBER	90888	NAME	A. J. Hill-Downing

INDEXED NAME

ADDRESS	CITY	STATE	ZIP
425 Belmont Avenue	Cincinnati	OH	45248

CREDIT RATING	1	CREDIT LIMIT	5000	BALANCE DUE	2980.00

Faunteroi's

[X] NEW [ ] CHANGE [ ] DELETE

ACCOUNT NUMBER	90998	NAME	Robert F. Alsage

INDEXED NAME

ADDRESS	CITY	STATE	ZIP
P.O. Box 1162	Aberdeen	OH	45101

CREDIT RATING	2	CREDIT LIMIT	1000	BALANCE DUE	163.89

Faunteroi's

[X] NEW [ ] CHANGE [ ] DELETE

ACCOUNT NUMBER	91000	NAME	Erin P. Savage

INDEXED NAME

ADDRESS	CITY	STATE	ZIP
1516 St. George Avenue	Fort Wayne	IN	46816

CREDIT RATING	1	CREDIT LIMIT	5000	BALANCE DUE	2403.00

Faunteroi's

☒ NEW ☐ CHANGE ☐ DELETE

ACCOUNT NUMBER	NAME
20202	R. Patrick Grogan

INDEXED NAME | | | | | | | | | | | | | | | | | | | | | | | |

ADDRESS	CITY	STATE	ZIP
456 Pico Boulevard	Dayton	OH	45406

CREDIT RATING	CREDIT LIMIT	BALANCE DUE
2	1000	0

Faunteroi's

☒ NEW ☐ CHANGE ☐ DELETE

ACCOUNT NUMBER	NAME
74592	Connie R. van der Pelt

INDEXED NAME | | | | | | | | | | | | | | | | | | | | | | | |

ADDRESS	CITY	STATE	ZIP
65 Southland Court	Cincinnati	OH	45232

CREDIT RATING	CREDIT LIMIT	BALANCE DUE
2	1000	451.92

Faunteroi's

☒ NEW ☐ CHANGE ☐ DELETE

ACCOUNT NUMBER	NAME
54901	Lou M. Alsake

INDEXED NAME | | | | | | | | | | | | | | | | | | | | | | | |

ADDRESS	CITY	STATE	ZIP
2456 Carrara Street	Dayton	OH	45410

CREDIT RATING	CREDIT LIMIT	BALANCE DUE
1	5000	396.00

Faunteroi's

☒ NEW ☐ CHANGE ☐ DELETE

ACCOUNT NUMBER	NAME
83023	Minoru Fujimura, M.D.

INDEXED NAME | | | | | | | | | | | | | | | | | | | | | | | |

ADDRESS	CITY	STATE	ZIP
541 High Street	Cincinnati	OH	45211

CREDIT RATING	CREDIT LIMIT	BALANCE DUE
2	1000	45.67

Faunteroi's

CUSTOMER ACCOUNT FORM

☐ NEW   ☒ CHANGE   ☐ DELETE

ACCOUNT NUMBER	26261	NAME	

INDEXED NAME																								

ADDRESS	356 Los Benots Drive	CITY	STATE	ZIP

CREDIT RATING	1	CREDIT LIMIT		BALANCE DUE	

Faunteroi's

CUSTOMER ACCOUNT FORM

☐ NEW   ☒ CHANGE   ☐ DELETE

ACCOUNT NUMBER		NAME	Jeron P. Sanders

INDEXED NAME																								

ADDRESS		CITY	STATE	ZIP

CREDIT RATING		CREDIT LIMIT		BALANCE DUE	581.29

Faunteroi's

CUSTOMER ACCOUNT FORM

☐ NEW   ☒ CHANGE   ☐ DELETE

ACCOUNT NUMBER		NAME	Martin G. McMichael

INDEXED NAME																								

ADDRESS		CITY	STATE	ZIP

CREDIT RATING		CREDIT LIMIT		BALANCE DUE	0

Faunteroi's

CUSTOMER ACCOUNT FORM

☐ NEW   ☒ CHANGE   ☐ DELETE

ACCOUNT NUMBER	34929	NAME	

INDEXED NAME																								

ADDRESS		CITY	STATE	ZIP

CREDIT RATING		CREDIT LIMIT	5000	BALANCE DUE	

Faunteroi's

☐ NEW ☐ CHANGE ☒ DELETE

ACCOUNT NUMBER	30272	NAME	

INDEXED NAME			

ADDRESS	CITY	STATE	ZIP

CREDIT RATING	CREDIT LIMIT	BALANCE DUE	

Faunteroi's

CUSTOMER ACCOUNT FORM 046

☐ NEW ☐ CHANGE ☒ DELETE

ACCOUNT NUMBER	38921	NAME	

INDEXED NAME			

ADDRESS	CITY	STATE	ZIP

CREDIT RATING	CREDIT LIMIT	BALANCE DUE	

Faunteroi's

CUSTOMER ACCOUNT FORM 047

☐ NEW ☐ CHANGE ☒ DELETE

ACCOUNT NUMBER	52973	NAME	

INDEXED NAME			

ADDRESS	CITY	STATE	ZIP

CREDIT RATING	CREDIT LIMIT	BALANCE DUE	

Faunteroi's

CUSTOMER ACCOUNT FORM 048

☐ NEW ☐ CHANGE ☒ DELETE

ACCOUNT NUMBER	84753	NAME	

INDEXED NAME			

ADDRESS	CITY	STATE	ZIP

CREDIT RATING	CREDIT LIMIT	BALANCE DUE	

Faunteroi's

☐ NEW   ☒ CHANGE   ☐ DELETE

ACCOUNT NUMBER	NAME
76405	

INDEXED NAME
| | | | | | | | | | | | | | | | | | | | | | | | | | |

ADDRESS	CITY	STATE	ZIP
452 Fremont Court	Charlestown	IN	47111-0254

CREDIT RATING	CREDIT LIMIT	BALANCE DUE

Faunteroi's

☐ NEW   ☒ CHANGE   ☐ DELETE

ACCOUNT NUMBER	NAME
34962	

INDEXED NAME
| | | | | | | | | | | | | | | | | | | | | | | | | | |

ADDRESS	CITY	STATE	ZIP
			47011-0719

CREDIT RATING	CREDIT LIMIT	BALANCE DUE
		672.89

Faunteroi's

☐ NEW   ☒ CHANGE   ☐ DELETE

ACCOUNT NUMBER	NAME
64656	Robert F. Alsage

INDEXED NAME
| | | | | | | | | | | | | | | | | | | | | | | | | | |

ADDRESS	CITY	STATE	ZIP
			45226-1727

CREDIT RATING	CREDIT LIMIT	BALANCE DUE
		158.73

Faunteroi's

☐ NEW   ☒ CHANGE   ☐ DELETE

ACCOUNT NUMBER	NAME
	G. Washington Smith

INDEXED NAME
| | | | | | | | | | | | | | | | | | | | | | | | | | |

ADDRESS	CITY	STATE	ZIP
			66012-0590

CREDIT RATING	CREDIT LIMIT	BALANCE DUE
2	1000	

Faunteroi's

CUSTOMER ACCOUNT FORM 053

[X] NEW   [ ] CHANGE   [ ] DELETE

ACCOUNT NUMBER	93256	NAME	Isaac A. Liebman		

INDEXED NAME

ADDRESS	CITY	STATE	ZIP
296 Wedgeworth Lane	Dayton	OH	45409

CREDIT RATING	1	CREDIT LIMIT	5000	BALANCE DUE	986.00

Faunteroi's

CUSTOMER ACCOUNT FORM 054

[X] NEW   [ ] CHANGE   [ ] DELETE

ACCOUNT NUMBER	93942	NAME	Corrine B. Reede		

INDEXED NAME

ADDRESS	CITY	STATE	ZIP
P.O. Box 6758	Reily	OH	45056

CREDIT RATING	1	CREDIT LIMIT	1000	BALANCE DUE	212.22

Faunteroi's

CUSTOMER ACCOUNT FORM 055

[X] NEW   [ ] CHANGE   [ ] DELETE

ACCOUNT NUMBER	90200	NAME	D'arcy Kim Cummings		

INDEXED NAME

ADDRESS	CITY	STATE	ZIP
251 James Street	Dayton	OH	45436

CREDIT RATING	3	CREDIT LIMIT	500	BALANCE DUE	33.89

Faunteroi's

CUSTOMER ACCOUNT FORM 056

[X] NEW   [ ] CHANGE   [ ] DELETE

ACCOUNT NUMBER	90710	NAME	Shawn T. O'Hara		

INDEXED NAME

ADDRESS	CITY	STATE	ZIP
2426 James Street	Cincinnati	OH	45240

CREDIT RATING	2	CREDIT LIMIT	1000	BALANCE DUE	456.87

UNIT II

QUANTUM CORPORATION EMPLOYEE FILE

For the next three units you will be employed by Quantum Corporation. Quantum is an organization that provides research services to many types of companies and agencies. Quantum is located in Eureka, California, and serves clients on the West Coast. Your job in this case study will be to design, create, and maintain Quantum's new computerized database files. The employee file will be developed in this unit, the client file in Unit III, and an equipment inventory file in Unit IV. These three files will be related in order to share the information in all the files; this will best meet the requirements of Quantum and its clients.

The human resources manager, Frank Mason, has asked all of the employees to complete a form furnishing information about themselves. The office manager, Alonzo Anduiza, has furnished additional information such as date of employment, method of wage payment, job title, and department in which the employee works.

Creating the File

Name _____   Date _____

Section _____   Evaluation _____

Note: Your instructor may tell you to skip this exercise if you are using the data diskette.

Using the information listed below, create the employee file for Quantum Corporation.

FIELD CONTENTS	FIELD NAME	LENGTH	TYPE
Social Security Number	SSNO	11	Character
Last Name	LNAME	12	Character
First Name	FNAME	12	Character
Middle Initial	MINITIAL	1	Character
Address	ADDRESS	25	Character
City	CITY	15	Character
State	STATE	2	Character
ZIP Code	ZIP	10	Character
Phone Number	PHONE	12	Character
Date Employed	DOE	8	Date
Wage Type	WTYPE	1	Character
Date of Birth	DOB	8	Date
Job Title	JTITLE	20	Character
Withholding Allowances	WITHALLOW	2	Numeric
Marital Status	MSTATUS	1	Character
Department	DEPT	8	Character

Note that in this file there are separate fields for the last name, first name, and middle initial. Because Quantum does not need to print its employees' names out in address form (first name, middle initial, last name), separate fields for the name and the indexed name are not necessary.

EXERCISE 23

Inputting Data From Forms 001 Through 028

Name _____   Date _____

Section _____   Evaluation _____

Note: Your instructor may tell you to skip this exercise if you are using the data diskette.

Remove employee input forms 001 through 028, pages 51 through 57. (Be sure to keep forms 029 through 032 for Exercise 27.) Key the data from each form field by field into the file. When entering the data for the **WTYPE** field, key:

- *C* for an employee paid by commission
- *H* for an employee paid hourly
- *S* for an employee paid a salaried wage.

For the data in the **MSTATUS** field, key:

- *M* for married employees
- *S* for single employees.

Note that dates are keyed in the format [yy.mm.dd]. For example, June 5, 1991, is entered [91.06.05]. This is done so the computer can arrange records according to date, if necessary.

EXERCISE 24

Listing the Entire File

Name _____   Date _____

Section _____   Evaluation _____

a. Make a hardcopy listing of Quantum's employee file. Your records should be listed in alphabetic order by the **LAST NAME** field. Use as few sheets of paper as possible for your printout.

b. After you have completed your listing, carefully proofread all records for errors and make corrections if necessary.

EXERCISE 25

Searching the File

Name _____   Date _____

Section _____   Evaluation _____

a. The CEO, Paula Woo, has asked you which employee in the sales department has been with the company the longest and when that person was employed.

Name: _____

Date Employed: _____

b. It is the first of the month (use the current month) and the human resources manager wants to know which employees have birthdays during this month in order to recognize their birthday with a card.

<u>Name</u>	<u>Date of Birth</u>
_____	_____
_____	_____
_____	_____
_____	_____

c. The accountant wants to know how many employees are paid an hourly wage. How many are there? _____

d. The accountant is auditing records and needs to know how many employees have claimed themselves as single on marital status and zero (0) on withholding allowances. How many? _____

EXERCISE 26

Listing Hourly Employees in the Research Department

Name _____   Date _____

Section _____   Evaluation _____

The research director, Eugene Adams, requests a listing of all employees in the research department who are paid hourly. Print a listing of their names in alphabetic order and include their date of employment.

EXERCISE 27

Adding New Employees

Name _____ Date _____

Section _____ Evaluation _____

The company has expanded operations and hired four new employees. Remove forms 029 through 032 on page 58, and add these records to the file. Write the current date on the forms in the **DOE** field.

EXERCISE 28

Making Some Changes

Name _____ Date _____

Section _____ Evaluation _____

Several employees have sent information to the human resources manager regarding changes to their records. Remove forms 033 through 036 on page 59 (Be sure to keep forms 037 through 040 for Exercise 33.), and update the file to include these changes.

EXERCISE 29

Finding the Salaried Employees

Name _____ Date _____

Section _____ Evaluation _____

Prepare a list of the name and department of each employee who is paid a salaried wage. The list should be in alphabetic order by the employee's last name. How many?

_____

42

EXERCISE 30

Answering Inquiries

Name _____ Date _____

Section _____ Evaluation _____

a. The company must report to its insurance agent the number of employees born after 1965 (65.12.31). Prepare a list showing their names and social security numbers. How many? _____

b. Employees with records of long service will be honored at the annual company dinner two months from now. In order to purchase the correct number of certificates and pins, the administrative assistant wants to know how many employees were hired by the company before 1965. How many? _____

EXERCISE 31

Finding Wage Information

Name _____ Date _____

Section _____ Evaluation _____

The accountant, Judy LeBlanc, would like to know:

a. How many employees are paid hourly? _____

b. How many employees are paid commissions? _____

c. How many employees are salaried? _____

QUANTUM CORPORATION EMPLOYEE FILE

EXERCISE

32 Reporting Names of Employees Nearing Retirement

Name _____ Date _____

Section _____ Evaluation _____

The office manager needs a report of all employees who were born before 1940. The fields to be included are: date of birth, name, date employed, and department. Report the records in order of the oldest to the youngest employee.

The title of the report is *EMPLOYEES NEAR RETIREMENT*. Use the following columnar titles: **DATE OF BIRTH, LAST NAME, FIRST NAME, M.I., DATE HIRED,** and **DEPT.**

EXERCISE

33 Changing Records

Name _____ Date _____

Section _____ Evaluation _____

An administrative assistant, Sarah Holmes, has sent you forms to make changes to existing records. Turn to page 60 and tear out forms 037 through 040, and update the records.

EXERCISE

34 Deleting Records

Name _____ Date _____

Section _____ Evaluation _____

Four employees have found new jobs outside the company. Remove forms 041 through 044 on page 61 (Be sure to keep forms 045 through 048 for Exercise 35.), and delete their records from the file.

EXERCISE 35

Making More Changes

Name _____ Date _____

Section _____ Evaluation _____

Turn to page 62, remove forms 045 through 048, and make the indicated changes to the file.

EXERCISE 36

Listing New Employees

Name _____ Date _____

Section _____ Evaluation _____

Four new people have been hired to replace the ones who left last week. Their employee input forms are on page 63, forms 049 through 052. Remove the forms, write the current date in the **DOE** field, and add the data to the file.

EXERCISE 37

Printing Research Department Employees

Name _____ Date _____

Section _____ Evaluation _____

The research director, Eugene Adams, has requested a listing in alphabetic order by last name of all the employees in the research department. List each name (last, first, and middle initial), wage type, and date hired.

EXERCISE

38

Finding an Employee

Name _____ Date _____

Section _____ Evaluation _____

The receptionist has a phone call for Marilyn Webb and needs to know in what department Marilyn works in order to transfer the call. What department?
_____

EXERCISE

39

Reporting Employees by Department

Name _____ Date _____

Section _____ Evaluation _____

The CEO has requested a report listing all employees by their department. The department names are to be listed in alphabetic order. If it is possible with your database program to sort on both a primary and a secondary field, print the names in alphabetic order within each department. The report should be in this format:

CURRENT EMPLOYEES BY DEPARTMENT

Department   Last Name   First Name   M.I.   Job Title

QUANTUM CORPORATION EMPLOYEE FILE

EXERCISE 40

Reporting the Sales Employees

Name _____ Date _____

Section _____ Evaluation _____

The new sales director, June Nelson, has asked for a report of all employees in that department. Index the file by job title as the primary key and the last name as the secondary key. Use this format:

SALES EMPLOYEES

Job Title   Last Name   First Name   M.I.   Social Security No.

EXERCISE 41

Changing Job Titles

Name _____ Date _____

Section _____ Evaluation _____

Eugene Adams would like to change the job title of all employees whose job title is *Research Asst.* to the new title, *Research Assoc.* Make the necessary changes.

EXERCISE 42

Listing Research Associates

Name _____ Date _____

Section _____ Evaluation _____

Print a list of all research associates in alphabetic order by last name. Include last name, first name, middle initial, date of employment, and social security number.

EXERCISE 43

Reporting All Employees by City

Name _____   Date _____

Section _____   Evaluation _____

The receptionist wants an up-to-date report of all employees by the city in which they live. Report the cities in alphabetic order and the names within each city in alphabetic order.

Use the following format:

```
CITY    LAST NAME    FIRST NAME  M.I.   PHONE NUMBER
```

EXERCISE 44

Changing Wage Type

Name _____   Date _____

Section _____   Evaluation _____

The CEO would like to convert the type of payment for the research associates from hourly to salaried. Make the necessary changes to the file.

EXERCISE 45

Changing Withholding Allowances

Name _____ Date _____

Section _____ Evaluation _____

Three employees are changing the number of exemptions they report for tax purposes. Change their records to the number of exemptions listed below:

EMPLOYEE	NEW NUMBER OF EXEMPTIONS
Marilyn Webb	2
Carlos Perez	3
Richard McCarty	1

EXERCISE 46

Finding the Number of Employees in Each Department

Name _____ Date _____

Section _____ Evaluation _____

The administration department has how many employees? _____

The research department has how many employees? _____

The sales department has how many employees? _____

EXERCISE 47

Changing Addresses

Name _____   Date _____

Section _____   Evaluation _____

Change the following employees' addresses:

EMPLOYEE	NEW ADDRESS
Frank Mason	114 Shore Drive
Joan Penland	5142 Mapledale Place

EXERCISE 48

Test— Quantum Corporation, Employee File

Your instructor will give you the test for this unit.

EMPLOYEE INPUT FORM — 001

Quantum Corporation

[X] EMPLOYED   [ ] CHANGE   [ ] TERMINATE

SOCIAL SECURITY NUMBER	LAST NAME	FIRST NAME	M.I.
112-39-6884	Woo	Paula	D

ADDRESS: 9147 Brentwood Drive

OFFICE USE ONLY

CITY	STATE	ZIP	DATE EMPLOYED	COMM. [ ] HOURLY [ ] SALARIED [X]
Eureka	CA	95501	87/01/30	

PHONE	DATE OF BIRTH	JOB TITLE
707-555-4158	49/02/09	CEO

WITHHOLDING ALLOWANCES	MARITAL STATUS	DEPARTMENT
2	M	Admin.

EMPLOYEE INPUT FORM — 002

Quantum Corporation

[X] EMPLOYED   [ ] CHANGE   [ ] TERMINATE

SOCIAL SECURITY NUMBER	LAST NAME	FIRST NAME	M.I.
122-44-8932	Crasnow	Jacob	B

ADDRESS: 2512 West Ridge Avenue

OFFICE USE ONLY

CITY	STATE	ZIP	DATE EMPLOYED	COMM. [ ] HOURLY [X] SALARIED [ ]
Bakersfield	CA	93301	91/01/11	

PHONE	DATE OF BIRTH	JOB TITLE
707-555-2196	68/03/14	Research Assistant.

WITHHOLDING ALLOWANCES	MARITAL STATUS	DEPARTMENT
0	S	Research

EMPLOYEE INPUT FORM — 003

Quantum Corporation

[X] EMPLOYED   [ ] CHANGE   [ ] TERMINATE

SOCIAL SECURITY NUMBER	LAST NAME	FIRST NAME	M.I.
202-43-5587	Webb	Marilyn	E

ADDRESS: 5125 Hobart Street

OFFICE USE ONLY

CITY	STATE	ZIP	DATE EMPLOYED	COMM. [ ] HOURLY [X] SALARIED [ ]
Eureka	CA	95501	87/01/15	

PHONE	DATE OF BIRTH	JOB TITLE
707-555-2915	67/10/17	Research Assistant

WITHHOLDING ALLOWANCES	MARITAL STATUS	DEPARTMENT
1	M	Research

EMPLOYEE INPUT FORM — 004

Quantum Corporation

[X] EMPLOYED   [ ] CHANGE   [ ] TERMINATE

SOCIAL SECURITY NUMBER	LAST NAME	FIRST NAME	M.I.
212-64-5088	Lawrence	John	T

ADDRESS: 4436 Tanglewood Road

OFFICE USE ONLY

CITY	STATE	ZIP	DATE EMPLOYED	COMM. [ ] HOURLY [ ] SALARIED [X]
Eureka	CA	95506	61/06/30	

PHONE	DATE OF BIRTH	JOB TITLE
707-555-8346	35/03/31	Sales Director

WITHHOLDING ALLOWANCES	MARITAL STATUS	DEPARTMENT
2	M	Sales

Quantum Corporation

EMPLOYEE INPUT FORM — 005

[X] EMPLOYED   [ ] CHANGE   [ ] TERMINATE

SOCIAL SECURITY NUMBER	LAST NAME	FIRST NAME	M.I.
221-50-4509	Pendergrass	Frank	T

ADDRESS: 273 Kings Mountain Road

OFFICE USE ONLY

CITY	STATE	ZIP	DATE EMPLOYED	COMM. / HOURLY / SALARIED
Bakersfield	CA	93306	91/01/15	COMM. [ ] HOURLY [X] SALARIED [ ]

PHONE	DATE OF BIRTH	JOB TITLE
707-555-2691	72/01/25	Research Assistant

WITHHOLDING ALLOWANCES	MARITAL STATUS	DEPARTMENT
1	S	Research

Quantum Corporation

EMPLOYEE INPUT FORM — 006

[X] EMPLOYED   [ ] CHANGE   [ ] TERMINATE

SOCIAL SECURITY NUMBER	LAST NAME	FIRST NAME	M.I.
223-88-2311	Lyle	George	E

ADDRESS: 3918 Chestnut Street

OFFICE USE ONLY

CITY	STATE	ZIP	DATE EMPLOYED	COMM. / HOURLY / SALARIED
Sacramento	CA	95814	85/07/01	COMM. [X] HOURLY [ ] SALARIED [ ]

PHONE	DATE OF BIRTH	JOB TITLE
707-555-4199	63/09/12	Client Rep.

WITHHOLDING ALLOWANCES	MARITAL STATUS	DEPARTMENT
0	S	Sales

Quantum Corporation

EMPLOYEE INPUT FORM — 007

[X] EMPLOYED   [ ] CHANGE   [ ] TERMINATE

SOCIAL SECURITY NUMBER	LAST NAME	FIRST NAME	M.I.
226-14-6679	Perez	Carlos	A

ADDRESS: 512 Stadium Road

OFFICE USE ONLY

CITY	STATE	ZIP	DATE EMPLOYED	COMM. / HOURLY / SALARIED
Sacramento	CA	95814	75/03/15	COMM. [ ] HOURLY [ ] SALARIED [X]

PHONE	DATE OF BIRTH	JOB TITLE
707-555-9149	55/08/18	Info. Resources Mgr.

WITHHOLDING ALLOWANCES	MARITAL STATUS	DEPARTMENT
2	M	Admin.

Quantum Corporation

EMPLOYEE INPUT FORM — 008

[X] EMPLOYED   [ ] CHANGE   [ ] TERMINATE

SOCIAL SECURITY NUMBER	LAST NAME	FIRST NAME	M.I.
229-35-6782	Turner	Carl	J

ADDRESS: 4581 Switchback Road

OFFICE USE ONLY

CITY	STATE	ZIP	DATE EMPLOYED	COMM. / HOURLY / SALARIED
Eureka	CA	95506	90/11/01	COMM. [ ] HOURLY [X] SALARIED [ ]

PHONE	DATE OF BIRTH	JOB TITLE
707-555-6169	70/11/15	Research Asst.

WITHHOLDING ALLOWANCES	MARITAL STATUS	DEPARTMENT
0	S	Research

EMPLOYEE INPUT FORM

Quantum Corporation

009

[X] EMPLOYED   [ ] CHANGE   [ ] TERMINATE

SOCIAL SECURITY NUMBER	LAST NAME	FIRST NAME	M.I.
230-11-6670	Green	Charles	S

ADDRESS
4698 Eastwood Lane

OFFICE USE ONLY

CITY	STATE	ZIP	DATE EMPLOYED	COMM. [ ] HOURLY [X] SALARIED [ ]
Eureka	CA	95514	88/08/29	

PHONE	DATE OF BIRTH	JOB TITLE
707-555-4048	70/03/25	Research Assistant

WITHHOLDING ALLOWANCES	MARITAL STATUS	DEPARTMENT
1	S	Research

EMPLOYEE INPUT FORM

Quantum Corporation

010

[X] EMPLOYED   [ ] CHANGE   [ ] TERMINATE

SOCIAL SECURITY NUMBER	LAST NAME	FIRST NAME	M.I.
230-16-6011	Webb	Estella	A

ADDRESS
6889 Edgewood Court

OFFICE USE ONLY

CITY	STATE	ZIP	DATE EMPLOYED	COMM. [ ] HOURLY [ ] SALARIED [X]
Bakersville	CA	93312	87/06/21	

PHONE	DATE OF BIRTH	JOB TITLE
707-555-9182	62/03/14	Comptroller

WITHHOLDING ALLOWANCES	MARITAL STATUS	DEPARTMENT
4	M	Admin.

EMPLOYEE INPUT FORM

Quantum Corporation

011

[X] EMPLOYED   [ ] CHANGE   [ ] TERMINATE

SOCIAL SECURITY NUMBER	LAST NAME	FIRST NAME	M.I.
230-88-6011	Tanner	Ruth	S

ADDRESS
442 Highland Avenue

OFFICE USE ONLY

CITY	STATE	ZIP	DATE EMPLOYED	COMM. [X] HOURLY [ ] SALARIED [ ]
Seattle	WA	98101	90/09/01	

PHONE	DATE OF BIRTH	JOB TITLE
619-555-8943	66/04/03	Client Rep.

WITHHOLDING ALLOWANCES	MARITAL STATUS	DEPARTMENT
1	S	Sales

EMPLOYEE INPUT FORM

Quantum Corporation

012

[X] EMPLOYED   [ ] CHANGE   [ ] TERMINATE

SOCIAL SECURITY NUMBER	LAST NAME	FIRST NAME	M.I.
231-46-9338	Hendrick	Ralph	H

ADDRESS
476 Midland Avenue

OFFICE USE ONLY

CITY	STATE	ZIP	DATE EMPLOYED	COMM. [ ] HOURLY [X] SALARIED [ ]
Santa Rosa	CA	95401	90/06/21	

PHONE	DATE OF BIRTH	JOB TITLE
707-555-1578	72/03/14	Research Asst.

WITHHOLDING ALLOWANCES	MARITAL STATUS	DEPARTMENT
1	S	Research

Quantum Corporation

EMPLOYEE INPUT FORM — 013

[X] EMPLOYED [ ] CHANGE [ ] TERMINATE

SOCIAL SECURITY NUMBER	LAST NAME	FIRST NAME	M.I.
231-64-6011	Price	Paul	W

ADDRESS: 62 Rockwell Road

OFFICE USE ONLY

CITY	STATE	ZIP	DATE EMPLOYED	COMM. [X] / HOURLY [ ] / SALARIED [ ]
Eureka	CA	95508	77/12/01	

PHONE	DATE OF BIRTH	JOB TITLE
707-555-1993	58/04/19	Client Rep.

WITHHOLDING ALLOWANCES	MARITAL STATUS	DEPARTMENT
2	M	Sales

Quantum Corporation

EMPLOYEE INPUT FORM — 014

[X] EMPLOYED [ ] CHANGE [ ] TERMINATE

SOCIAL SECURITY NUMBER	LAST NAME	FIRST NAME	M.I.
232-11-7743	McCarty	Richard	M

ADDRESS: 1162 Homestead Avenue

OFFICE USE ONLY

CITY	STATE	ZIP	DATE EMPLOYED	COMM. [ ] / HOURLY [ ] / SALARIED [X]
Eureka	CA	95506	90/04/21	

PHONE	DATE OF BIRTH	JOB TITLE
707-555-0072	70/01/30	Bookkeeping Clerk

WITHHOLDING ALLOWANCES	MARITAL STATUS	DEPARTMENT
2	M	Admin.

Quantum Corporation

EMPLOYEE INPUT FORM — 015

[X] EMPLOYED [ ] CHANGE [ ] TERMINATE

SOCIAL SECURITY NUMBER	LAST NAME	FIRST NAME	M.I.
233-16-9456	Adams	Eugene	E

ADDRESS: 633 Fernwood Drive

OFFICE USE ONLY

CITY	STATE	ZIP	DATE EMPLOYED	COMM. [ ] / HOURLY [ ] / SALARIED [X]
Eureka	CA	95510	84/03/10	

PHONE	DATE OF BIRTH	JOB TITLE
619-555-8371	59/08/27	Research Director

WITHHOLDING ALLOWANCES	MARITAL STATUS	DEPARTMENT
1	S	Research

Quantum Corporation

EMPLOYEE INPUT FORM — 016

[X] EMPLOYED [ ] CHANGE [ ] TERMINATE

SOCIAL SECURITY NUMBER	LAST NAME	FIRST NAME	M.I.
239-23-7082	Mason	Frank	P

ADDRESS: 1677 Riverview Road

OFFICE USE ONLY

CITY	STATE	ZIP	DATE EMPLOYED	COMM. [ ] / HOURLY [ ] / SALARIED [X]
Santa Rosa	CA	95410	89/04/01	

PHONE	DATE OF BIRTH	JOB TITLE
707-555-9146	37/11/13	Human Resources Mgr.

WITHHOLDING ALLOWANCES	MARITAL STATUS	DEPARTMENT
1	S	Admin.

EMPLOYEE INPUT FORM — 017

Quantum Corporation

[X] EMPLOYED [ ] CHANGE [ ] TERMINATE

SOCIAL SECURITY NUMBER	LAST NAME	FIRST NAME	M.I.
461-25-2998	Anduiza	Alonzo	H

ADDRESS: 2982 Oxford Street

OFFICE USE ONLY

CITY	STATE	ZIP	DATE EMPLOYED	COMM. [ ] HOURLY [ ] SALARIED [X]
Eureka	CA	95509	87/09/19	

PHONE	DATE OF BIRTH	JOB TITLE
707-555-2700	50/08/17	Office Mgr.

WITHHOLDING ALLOWANCES	MARITAL STATUS	DEPARTMENT
3	M	Admin.

EMPLOYEE INPUT FORM — 018

Quantum Corporation

[X] EMPLOYED [ ] CHANGE [ ] TERMINATE

SOCIAL SECURITY NUMBER	LAST NAME	FIRST NAME	M.I.
612-23-8993	Farmer	Michael	B

ADDRESS: 4629 Boxwood Lane

OFFICE USE ONLY

CITY	STATE	ZIP	DATE EMPLOYED	COMM. [ ] HOURLY [X] SALARIED [ ]
Sacramento	CA	95803	89/08/11	

PHONE	DATE OF BIRTH	JOB TITLE
707-555-2906	65/04/19	Research Asst.

WITHHOLDING ALLOWANCES	MARITAL STATUS	DEPARTMENT
3	M	Research

EMPLOYEE INPUT FORM — 019

Quantum Corporation

[X] EMPLOYED [ ] CHANGE [ ] TERMINATE

SOCIAL SECURITY NUMBER	LAST NAME	FIRST NAME	M.I.
640-13-2296	Holmes	Sarah	C

ADDRESS: 303 Maple Street

OFFICE USE ONLY

CITY	STATE	ZIP	DATE EMPLOYED	COMM. [ ] HOURLY [ ] SALARIED [X]
Santa Rosa	CA	95408	82/03/19	

PHONE	DATE OF BIRTH	JOB TITLE
619-555-2762	55/11/21	Administrative Asst.

WITHHOLDING ALLOWANCES	MARITAL STATUS	DEPARTMENT
0	S	Admin.

EMPLOYEE INPUT FORM — 020

Quantum Corporation

[X] EMPLOYED [ ] CHANGE [ ] TERMINATE

SOCIAL SECURITY NUMBER	LAST NAME	FIRST NAME	M.I.
770-53-1266	Penland	Joan	J

ADDRESS: 5169 Mapledale Place

OFFICE USE ONLY

CITY	STATE	ZIP	DATE EMPLOYED	COMM. [ ] HOURLY [X] SALARIED [ ]
Bakersfield	CA	93312	90/03/25	

PHONE	DATE OF BIRTH	JOB TITLE
707-555-9143	71/02/14	Research Asst.

WITHHOLDING ALLOWANCES	MARITAL STATUS	DEPARTMENT
1	M	Research

Quantum Corporation

EMPLOYEE INPUT FORM — 021

[X] EMPLOYED   [ ] CHANGE   [ ] TERMINATE

SOCIAL SECURITY NUMBER	332-68-7721
LAST NAME	Treat
FIRST NAME	Porter
M.I.	L
ADDRESS	241 Greenwood Lane
CITY	Los Angeles
STATE	CA
ZIP	90015
PHONE	213-555-2714
DATE OF BIRTH	65/05/23
WITHHOLDING ALLOWANCES	0
MARITAL STATUS	S

OFFICE USE ONLY

DATE EMPLOYED	90/11/05
COMM.	[X]
HOURLY	[ ]
SALARIED	[ ]
JOB TITLE	Client Rep.
DEPARTMENT	Sales

EMPLOYEE INPUT FORM — 022

[X] EMPLOYED   [ ] CHANGE   [ ] TERMINATE

SOCIAL SECURITY NUMBER	341-12-6672
LAST NAME	LeBlanc
FIRST NAME	Judy
M.I.	D
ADDRESS	1193 Hilltop Road
CITY	Eureka
STATE	CA
ZIP	95501
PHONE	707-555-4049
DATE OF BIRTH	46/04/22
WITHHOLDING ALLOWANCES	4
MARITAL STATUS	M

OFFICE USE ONLY

DATE EMPLOYED	65/06/15
COMM.	[ ]
HOURLY	[ ]
SALARIED	[X]
JOB TITLE	Accountant
DEPARTMENT	Admin.

EMPLOYEE INPUT FORM — 023

[X] EMPLOYED   [ ] CHANGE   [ ] TERMINATE

SOCIAL SECURITY NUMBER	341-46-9338
LAST NAME	Holmes
FIRST NAME	Stephen
M.I.	M
ADDRESS	1291 Parkview Avenue
CITY	San Francisco
STATE	CA
ZIP	94120
PHONE	415-555-0382
DATE OF BIRTH	53/04/07
WITHHOLDING ALLOWANCES	1
MARITAL STATUS	S

OFFICE USE ONLY

DATE EMPLOYED	85/10/01
COMM.	[X]
HOURLY	[ ]
SALARIED	[ ]
JOB TITLE	Client Rep.
DEPARTMENT	Sales

EMPLOYEE INPUT FORM — 024

[X] EMPLOYED   [ ] CHANGE   [ ] TERMINATE

SOCIAL SECURITY NUMBER	343-28-6632
LAST NAME	Goldblatz
FIRST NAME	Clara
M.I.	R
ADDRESS	351 Brandon Drive
CITY	Bakersfield
STATE	CA
ZIP	93310
PHONE	707-555-2162
DATE OF BIRTH	61/04/30
WITHHOLDING ALLOWANCES	0
MARITAL STATUS	M

OFFICE USE ONLY

DATE EMPLOYED	91/01/17
COMM.	[ ]
HOURLY	[ ]
SALARIED	[X]
JOB TITLE	Receptionist
DEPARTMENT	Admin.

Quantum Corporation — EMPLOYEE INPUT FORM — 025

[X] EMPLOYED [ ] CHANGE [ ] TERMINATE

SOCIAL SECURITY NUMBER	LAST NAME	FIRST NAME	M.I.
412-68-8997	Eberhard	Dorris	W

ADDRESS: 698 Catskill Avenue

OFFICE USE ONLY

CITY	STATE	ZIP
San Diego	CA	92110

DATE EMPLOYED	COMM. [X] HOURLY [ ] SALARIED [ ]
76/06/20	

PHONE	DATE OF BIRTH
619-555-5172	54/02/26

JOB TITLE: Client Rep.

WITHHOLDING ALLOWANCES	MARITAL STATUS
1	M

DEPARTMENT: Sales

Quantum Corporation — EMPLOYEE INPUT FORM — 026

[X] EMPLOYED [ ] CHANGE [ ] TERMINATE

SOCIAL SECURITY NUMBER	LAST NAME	FIRST NAME	M.I.
422-23-8870	Abernathy	Daniel	A

ADDRESS: 1536 Circle Brook Drive

OFFICE USE ONLY

CITY	STATE	ZIP
Santa Rosa	CA	95404

DATE EMPLOYED	COMM. [ ] HOURLY [ ] SALARIED [X]
72/01/25	

PHONE	DATE OF BIRTH
707-555-0733	50/03/17

JOB TITLE: Statistician

WITHHOLDING ALLOWANCES	MARITAL STATUS
1	S

DEPARTMENT: Research

Quantum Corporation — EMPLOYEE INPUT FORM — 027

[X] EMPLOYED [ ] CHANGE [ ] TERMINATE

SOCIAL SECURITY NUMBER	LAST NAME	FIRST NAME	M.I.
441-66-2099	Janosko	Marie	H

ADDRESS: 1168 Lawrence Avenue

OFFICE USE ONLY

CITY	STATE	ZIP
Bakersfield	CA	93311

DATE EMPLOYED	COMM. [ ] HOURLY [X] SALARIED [ ]
85/07/15	

PHONE	DATE OF BIRTH
619-555-6188	59/09/18

JOB TITLE: Research Asst.

WITHHOLDING ALLOWANCES	MARITAL STATUS
1	S

DEPARTMENT: Research

Quantum Corporation — EMPLOYEE INPUT FORM — 028

[X] EMPLOYED [ ] CHANGE [ ] TERMINATE

SOCIAL SECURITY NUMBER	LAST NAME	FIRST NAME	M.I.
459-23-6680	DiAngelo	Mario	C

ADDRESS: 141 South Main Street

OFFICE USE ONLY

CITY	STATE	ZIP
Eureka	CA	95513

DATE EMPLOYED	COMM. [ ] HOURLY [X] SALARIED [ ]
90/11/01	

PHONE	DATE OF BIRTH
707-555-2496	60/02/25

JOB TITLE: Research Asst.

WITHHOLDING ALLOWANCES	MARITAL STATUS
1	M

DEPARTMENT: Research

EMPLOYEE INPUT FORM 029

Quantum Corporation

[X] EMPLOYED [ ] CHANGE [ ] TERMINATE

SOCIAL SECURITY NUMBER	LAST NAME	FIRST NAME	M.I.
260-98-1288	Basham	Jerome	M

ADDRESS
161 Capewell Avenue

OFFICE USE ONLY

CITY	STATE	ZIP	DATE EMPLOYED	COMM. [ ] HOURLY [X] SALARIED [ ]
Sacramento	CA	95814		

PHONE	DATE OF BIRTH	JOB TITLE
707-555-7088	67/06/01	Research Asst.

WITHHOLDING ALLOWANCES	MARITAL STATUS	DEPARTMENT
1	S	Research

EMPLOYEE INPUT FORM 030

Quantum Corporation

[X] EMPLOYED [ ] CHANGE [ ] TERMINATE

SOCIAL SECURITY NUMBER	LAST NAME	FIRST NAME	M.I.
312-68-9114	Levinson	Wayne	A

ADDRESS
8400 Hampton Court Place

OFFICE USE ONLY

CITY	STATE	ZIP	DATE EMPLOYED	COMM. [ ] HOURLY [ ] SALARIED [X]
Bakersfield	CA	93314		

PHONE	DATE OF BIRTH	JOB TITLE
707-555-1129	44/12/21	Accountant

WITHHOLDING ALLOWANCES	MARITAL STATUS	DEPARTMENT
2	M	Admin.

EMPLOYEE INPUT FORM 031

Quantum Corporation

[X] EMPLOYED [ ] CHANGE [ ] TERMINATE

SOCIAL SECURITY NUMBER	LAST NAME	FIRST NAME	M.I.
313-99-1286	Nelson	Jane	A

ADDRESS
227 Sawmill Road

OFFICE USE ONLY

CITY	STATE	ZIP	DATE EMPLOYED	COMM. [X] HOURLY [ ] SALARIED [ ]
Spokane	WA	99206		

PHONE	DATE OF BIRTH	JOB TITLE
509-555-8127	62/09/29	Client Rep.

WITHHOLDING ALLOWANCES	MARITAL STATUS	DEPARTMENT
0	S	Sales

EMPLOYEE INPUT FORM 032

Quantum Corporation

[X] EMPLOYED [ ] CHANGE [ ] TERMINATE

SOCIAL SECURITY NUMBER	LAST NAME	FIRST NAME	M.I.
332-61-1689	Weber	Leslee	G

ADDRESS
198 Woodview Road

OFFICE USE ONLY

CITY	STATE	ZIP	DATE EMPLOYED	COMM. [ ] HOURLY [X] SALARIED [ ]
Santa Rosa	CA	95403		

PHONE	DATE OF BIRTH	JOB TITLE
707-555-0082	60/07/23	Research Asst.

WITHHOLDING ALLOWANCES	MARITAL STATUS	DEPARTMENT
2	M	Research

EMPLOYEE INPUT FORM   033

Quantum
Corporation

☐ EMPLOYED   ☒ CHANGE   ☐ TERMINATE

SOCIAL SECURITY NUMBER 202-43-5587	LAST NAME		FIRST NAME	M.I.

ADDRESS			**OFFICE USE ONLY**	
CITY	STATE	ZIP	DATE EMPLOYED	COMM. ☐ HOURLY ☐ SALARIED ☐
PHONE 707-555-3105	DATE OF BIRTH		JOB TITLE	
WITHHOLDING ALLOWANCES	MARITAL STATUS		DEPARTMENT	

EMPLOYEE INPUT FORM   034

Quantum
Corporation

☐ EMPLOYED   ☒ CHANGE   ☐ TERMINATE

SOCIAL SECURITY NUMBER 230-88-6011	LAST NAME Sharpe		FIRST NAME	M.I. T

ADDRESS			**OFFICE USE ONLY**	
CITY	STATE	ZIP	DATE EMPLOYED	COMM. ☐ HOURLY ☐ SALARIED ☐
PHONE	DATE OF BIRTH		JOB TITLE	
WITHHOLDING ALLOWANCES	MARITAL STATUS M		DEPARTMENT	

EMPLOYEE INPUT FORM   035

Quantum
Corporation

☐ EMPLOYED   ☒ CHANGE   ☐ TERMINATE

SOCIAL SECURITY NUMBER 239-23-7082	LAST NAME		FIRST NAME	M.I.

ADDRESS 12101 Sycamore Street			**OFFICE USE ONLY**	
CITY	STATE	ZIP	DATE EMPLOYED	COMM. ☐ HOURLY ☐ SALARIED ☐
PHONE	DATE OF BIRTH		JOB TITLE	
WITHHOLDING ALLOWANCES	MARITAL STATUS		DEPARTMENT	

EMPLOYEE INPUT FORM   036

Quantum
Corporation

☐ EMPLOYED   ☒ CHANGE   ☐ TERMINATE

SOCIAL SECURITY NUMBER 212-64-5088	LAST NAME		FIRST NAME	M.I.

ADDRESS 2121 Brandon Avenue			**OFFICE USE ONLY**	
CITY	STATE	ZIP	DATE EMPLOYED	COMM. ☐ HOURLY ☐ SALARIED ☐
PHONE 707-555-1492	DATE OF BIRTH		JOB TITLE	
WITHHOLDING ALLOWANCES	MARITAL STATUS		DEPARTMENT	

Form 037

Quantum Corporation

EMPLOYEE INPUT FORM   037

[ ] EMPLOYED   [X] CHANGE   [ ] TERMINATE

SOCIAL SECURITY NUMBER	LAST NAME	FIRST NAME	M.I.
233-16-9456			

ADDRESS	**OFFICE USE ONLY**

CITY	STATE	ZIP	DATE EMPLOYED	COMM. [ ] HOURLY [ ] SALARIED [ ]

PHONE	DATE OF BIRTH	JOB TITLE

WITHHOLDING ALLOWANCES	MARITAL STATUS	DEPARTMENT
2	M	

Form 038

Quantum Corporation

EMPLOYEE INPUT FORM   038

[ ] EMPLOYED   [X] CHANGE   [ ] TERMINATE

SOCIAL SECURITY NUMBER	LAST NAME	FIRST NAME	M.I.
640-13-2296			

ADDRESS	**OFFICE USE ONLY**
2226 New Castle Drive	

CITY	STATE	ZIP	DATE EMPLOYED	COMM. [ ] HOURLY [ ] SALARIED [ ]

PHONE	DATE OF BIRTH	JOB TITLE
707-555-2771		

WITHHOLDING ALLOWANCES	MARITAL STATUS	DEPARTMENT

Form 039

Quantum Corporation

EMPLOYEE INPUT FORM   039

[ ] EMPLOYED   [X] CHANGE   [ ] TERMINATE

SOCIAL SECURITY NUMBER	LAST NAME	FIRST NAME	M.I.
343-28-6632			

ADDRESS	**OFFICE USE ONLY**

CITY	STATE	ZIP	DATE EMPLOYED	COMM. [ ] HOURLY [ ] SALARIED [ ]

PHONE	DATE OF BIRTH	JOB TITLE

WITHHOLDING ALLOWANCES	MARITAL STATUS	DEPARTMENT
	S	

Form 040

Quantum Corporation

EMPLOYEE INPUT FORM   040

[ ] EMPLOYED   [X] CHANGE   [ ] TERMINATE

SOCIAL SECURITY NUMBER	LAST NAME	FIRST NAME	M.I.
232-11-7743			

ADDRESS	**OFFICE USE ONLY**

CITY	STATE	ZIP	DATE EMPLOYED	COMM. [ ] HOURLY [ ] SALARIED [ ]

PHONE	DATE OF BIRTH	JOB TITLE
707-555-1492		

WITHHOLDING ALLOWANCES	MARITAL STATUS	DEPARTMENT
3		

EMPLOYEE INPUT FORM

Quantum Corporation

041

☐ EMPLOYED   ☐ CHANGE   ☒ TERMINATE

SOCIAL SECURITY NUMBER 212-64-5088	LAST NAME	FIRST NAME	M.I.

ADDRESS		**OFFICE USE ONLY**	
CITY	STATE	ZIP	DATE EMPLOYED	COMM. ☐ HOURLY ☐ SALARIED ☐
PHONE	DATE OF BIRTH		JOB TITLE	
WITHHOLDING ALLOWANCES	MARITAL STATUS		DEPARTMENT	

EMPLOYEE INPUT FORM

Quantum Corporation

042

☐ EMPLOYED   ☐ CHANGE   ☒ TERMINATE

SOCIAL SECURITY NUMBER 332-61-1689	LAST NAME	FIRST NAME	M.I.

ADDRESS		**OFFICE USE ONLY**	
CITY	STATE	ZIP	DATE EMPLOYED	COMM. ☐ HOURLY ☐ SALARIED ☐
PHONE	DATE OF BIRTH		JOB TITLE	
WITHHOLDING ALLOWANCES	MARITAL STATUS		DEPARTMENT	

EMPLOYEE INPUT FORM

Quantum Corporation

043

☐ EMPLOYED   ☐ CHANGE   ☒ TERMINATE

SOCIAL SECURITY NUMBER 459-23-6680	LAST NAME	FIRST NAME	M.I.

ADDRESS		**OFFICE USE ONLY**	
CITY	STATE	ZIP	DATE EMPLOYED	COMM. ☐ HOURLY ☐ SALARIED ☐
PHONE	DATE OF BIRTH		JOB TITLE	
WITHHOLDING ALLOWANCES	MARITAL STATUS		DEPARTMENT	

EMPLOYEE INPUT FORM

Quantum Corporation

044

☐ EMPLOYED   ☐ CHANGE   ☒ TERMINATE

SOCIAL SECURITY NUMBER 422-23-8870	LAST NAME	FIRST NAME	M.I.

ADDRESS		**OFFICE USE ONLY**	
CITY	STATE	ZIP	DATE EMPLOYED	COMM. ☐ HOURLY ☐ SALARIED ☐
PHONE	DATE OF BIRTH		JOB TITLE	
WITHHOLDING ALLOWANCES	MARITAL STATUS		DEPARTMENT	

Quantum Corporation

EMPLOYEE INPUT FORM 045

☐ EMPLOYED   ☒ CHANGE   ☐ TERMINATE

SOCIAL SECURITY NUMBER	LAST NAME	FIRST NAME	M.I.
202-43-5587			

ADDRESS			

OFFICE USE ONLY

CITY	STATE	ZIP	DATE EMPLOYED	COMM. ☐ HOURLY ☐ SALARIED ☐

PHONE	DATE OF BIRTH	JOB TITLE
707-555-5167		

WITHHOLDING ALLOWANCES	MARITAL STATUS	DEPARTMENT

Quantum Corporation

EMPLOYEE INPUT FORM 046

☐ EMPLOYED   ☒ CHANGE   ☐ TERMINATE

SOCIAL SECURITY NUMBER	LAST NAME	FIRST NAME	M.I.
223-88-2311			

ADDRESS			

OFFICE USE ONLY

CITY	STATE	ZIP	DATE EMPLOYED	COMM. ☐ HOURLY ☐ SALARIED ☐

PHONE	DATE OF BIRTH	JOB TITLE

WITHHOLDING ALLOWANCES	MARITAL STATUS	DEPARTMENT
1	M	

Quantum Corporation

EMPLOYEE INPUT FORM 047

☐ EMPLOYED   ☒ CHANGE   ☐ TERMINATE

SOCIAL SECURITY NUMBER	LAST NAME	FIRST NAME	M.I.
412-68-8997			

ADDRESS			

OFFICE USE ONLY

CITY	STATE	ZIP	DATE EMPLOYED	COMM. ☐ HOURLY ☐ SALARIED ☐

PHONE	DATE OF BIRTH	JOB TITLE
619-555-9180		

WITHHOLDING ALLOWANCES	MARITAL STATUS	DEPARTMENT

Quantum Corporation

EMPLOYEE INPUT FORM 048

☐ EMPLOYED   ☒ CHANGE   ☐ TERMINATE

SOCIAL SECURITY NUMBER	LAST NAME	FIRST NAME	M.I.
231-46-9338			

ADDRESS			
1436 Spring Hill Drive			

OFFICE USE ONLY

CITY	STATE	ZIP	DATE EMPLOYED	COMM. ☐ HOURLY ☐ SALARIED ☐

PHONE	DATE OF BIRTH	JOB TITLE
707-555-9632		

WITHHOLDING ALLOWANCES	MARITAL STATUS	DEPARTMENT
	M	

EMPLOYEE INPUT FORM 049

Quantum Corporation

[X] EMPLOYED [ ] CHANGE [ ] TERMINATE

SOCIAL SECURITY NUMBER	LAST NAME	FIRST NAME	M.I.
412-62-3310	Germaine	Paul	F

ADDRESS
4572 Wycomb Lane

OFFICE USE ONLY

CITY	STATE	ZIP	DATE EMPLOYED	COMM. [ ] HOURLY [X] SALARIED [ ]
Bakersfield	CA	93308		

PHONE	DATE OF BIRTH	JOB TITLE
707-555-4219	67/01/28	Research Asst.

WITHHOLDING ALLOWANCES	MARITAL STATUS	DEPARTMENT
0	S	Research

EMPLOYEE INPUT FORM 050

Quantum Corporation

[X] EMPLOYED [ ] CHANGE [ ] TERMINATE

SOCIAL SECURITY NUMBER	LAST NAME	FIRST NAME	M.I.
502-68-6632	Nelson	June	C

ADDRESS
239 West View Place

OFFICE USE ONLY

CITY	STATE	ZIP	DATE EMPLOYED	COMM. [ ] HOURLY [ ] SALARIED [X]
Santa Rosa	CA	95404		

PHONE	DATE OF BIRTH	JOB TITLE
707-555-4187	59/03/25	Sales Director

WITHHOLDING ALLOWANCES	MARITAL STATUS	DEPARTMENT
2	M	Sales

EMPLOYEE INPUT FORM 051

Quantum Corporation

[X] EMPLOYED [ ] CHANGE [ ] TERMINATE

SOCIAL SECURITY NUMBER	LAST NAME	FIRST NAME	M.I.
314-14-6951	Rodriguez	Juan	M

ADDRESS
41 Sandy Lane

OFFICE USE ONLY

CITY	STATE	ZIP	DATE EMPLOYED	COMM. [X] HOURLY [ ] SALARIED [ ]
Sacramento	CA	95812		

PHONE	DATE OF BIRTH	JOB TITLE
707-555-1192	60/08/17	Research Asst.

WITHHOLDING ALLOWANCES	MARITAL STATUS	DEPARTMENT
0	M	Research

EMPLOYEE INPUT FORM 052

Quantum Corporation

[X] EMPLOYED [ ] CHANGE [ ] TERMINATE

SOCIAL SECURITY NUMBER	LAST NAME	FIRST NAME	M.I.
342-88-1003	Waske	Paul	P

ADDRESS
20022 Plaza Lake Drive

OFFICE USE ONLY

CITY	STATE	ZIP	DATE EMPLOYED	COMM. [ ] HOURLY [ ] SALARIED [X]
Bakersfield	CA	93308		

PHONE	DATE OF BIRTH	JOB TITLE
707-555-2127	52/10/03	Statistician

WITHHOLDING ALLOWANCES	MARITAL STATUS	DEPARTMENT
4	M	Research

QUANTUM CORPORATION CLIENT FILE

As part of its research services, Quantum Corporation tests and evaluates products, services, and promotional ideas for its clients. Clients of Quantum include businesses, government agencies, and other organizations such as schools and nonprofit charities.

The management team of Quantum has decided to convert all client records from a card file to a computerized file; this will be the second file in the Quantum database. Your job is to design the client file, place the current client records in it, and maintain the file as changes occur.

In Unit I, Faunteroi's customer file, all of the names in the file were names of people. Before you created the file, you learned how to enter their names into the file in two ways: standard form and indexed form. However, in the client file of Quantum Corporation all the names in the file are names of businesses, government agencies, or other organizations.

Names of businesses, government agencies, and other organizations may also be entered into computer files in two ways:

1. In *letterhead* form, the way the name usually appears on letterheads, advertisements, and other documents that are seen by those with whom the organization does business; for example:

    The Wright-Zorn Company

2. In *indexed* form, the way the name would be looked up in a directory that is arranged alphabetically; for example:

    WRIGHTZORN COMPANY THE

When you set up the computerized client file for Quantum, you will enter the name of each client twice; once in letterhead form and once in indexed form. You will be given each client's name in letterhead form. It will be your job to determine the indexed form. Exercises 49A, 49B, 50A, and 50B will give you practice in indexing names of businesses, government agencies, and other organizations.

Name _____   Date _____

Section _____   Evaluation _____

STUDY THE INDEXING RULE

Business and organization names are indexed as written. Each unit in the name is to be considered, including prepositions, conjunctions, and articles. The only exception is when the word *the* is the first unit in the name. In this case, *the* is the last filing unit. Radio- and television-station call letters are considered to be one unit.

LETTERHEAD FORM	INDEXED FORM
The Barnacle Restaurant	BARNACLE RESTAURANT THE
Center for the Performing Arts	CENTER FOR THE PERFORMING ARTS
Garnett and Sons Milling	GARNETT AND SONS MILLING
John Norman Clothing Company	JOHN NORMAN CLOTHING COMPANY*
New York Carpet World	NEW YORK CARPET WORLD
Pendleton of Georgetown	PENDLETON OF GEORGETOWN
RDI Corporation	RDI CORPORATION
TJ Company	TJ COMPANY
WXTE TV	WXTE TV
WYCI Radio	WYCI RADIO

* Note that the name *John Norman* is not transposed. This is because it is part of thebusiness name.

PRACTICE INDEXING

Write each name in indexed form as shown in the example.

0.   The Brush and Easel Company

|B|R|U|S|H| |A|N|D| |E|A|S|E|L| |C|O|M|P|A|N|Y| |T|H|E| | |

1.   Carson and Carson Tax Service

| | | | | | | | | | | | | | | | | | | | | | | | | | | | | | | | | | | |

2.   Connie Williams Cooking School

| | | | | | | | | | | | | | | | | | | | | | | | | | | | | | | | | | | |

3.   The Dungeon Costume Store

| | | | | | | | | | | | | | | | | | | | | | | | | | | | | | | | | | | |

4.   E G Corporation

| | | | | | | | | | | | | | | | | | | | | | | | | | | | | | | | | | | |

5.   HJR Investors

|_|_|_|_|_|_|_|_|_|_|_|_|_|_|_|_|_|_|_|_|_|_|_|_|_|_|_|_|_|_|_|_|_|_|_|_|_|_|_|

6.   Stafford of Wales Seafood

|_|_|_|_|_|_|_|_|_|_|_|_|_|_|_|_|_|_|_|_|_|_|_|_|_|_|_|_|_|_|_|_|_|_|_|_|_|_|_|

7.   West Virginia Coal Company

|_|_|_|_|_|_|_|_|_|_|_|_|_|_|_|_|_|_|_|_|_|_|_|_|_|_|_|_|_|_|_|_|_|_|_|_|_|_|_|

8.   WRVA Radio

|_|_|_|_|_|_|_|_|_|_|_|_|_|_|_|_|_|_|_|_|_|_|_|_|_|_|_|_|_|_|_|_|_|_|_|_|_|_|_|

9.   WWVA Radio

|_|_|_|_|_|_|_|_|_|_|_|_|_|_|_|_|_|_|_|_|_|_|_|_|_|_|_|_|_|_|_|_|_|_|_|_|_|_|_|

10.   Z and A Trucking Company

|_|_|_|_|_|_|_|_|_|_|_|_|_|_|_|_|_|_|_|_|_|_|_|_|_|_|_|_|_|_|_|_|_|_|_|_|_|_|_|

Indexing Business and Organization Names With Punctuation

Name _____ Date _____

Section _____ Evaluation _____

STUDY THE INDEXING RULE

Omit all punctuation when indexing. This includes periods, commas, dashes, hyphens, and apostrophes. Hyphenated words are considered to be one unit.

LETTERHEAD FORM

Afton Mountain Gifts, Inc.
Buzzi's Antiques
Clifton-Brown Insurance
D-J-R Fixin's
Ellis, Dorn, and Wood Attorneys
Frieda Wheat-Skully Tax Service
St. Paul's College
The Victorian Art-Barn

INDEXED FORM

AFTON MOUNTAIN GIFTS INC
BUZZIS ANTIQUES
CLIFTONBROWN INSURANCE
DJR FIXINS
ELLIS DORN AND WOOD ATTORNEYS
FRIEDA WHEATSKULLY TAX SERVICE
STPAULS COLLEGE*
VICTORIAN ARTBARN THE

* Note that the prefix *St.* is written in indexed form without the period or space after it, as is the case with a personal-name prefix.

PRACTICE INDEXING

0. Alp-Suisse Child's Corner

    |A|L|P|S|U|I|S|S|E| |C|H|I|L|D|S| |C|O|R|N|E|R| | | | | | |

1. Antonio's Car Care

    | | | | | | | | | | | | | | | | | | | | | | | | | | | | | | |

2. Carolina Investors, Inc.

    | | | | | | | | | | | | | | | | | | | | | | | | | | | | | | |

3. Carolina-Wrey Pharmacy

    | | | | | | | | | | | | | | | | | | | | | | | | | | | | | | |

4. C-H Wishin'-Well Eats

    | | | | | | | | | | | | | | | | | | | | | | | | | | | | | | |

5.   Clyde, Bill, and Annie's Band

|_|_|_|_|_|_|_|_|_|_|_|_|_|_|_|_|_|_|_|_|_|_|_|_|_|_|_|_|_|_|_|_|_|_|_|_|

6.   Mary Lyles-Keen Exterminators

|_|_|_|_|_|_|_|_|_|_|_|_|_|_|_|_|_|_|_|_|_|_|_|_|_|_|_|_|_|_|_|_|_|_|_|_|

7.   St. James' Conservatory

|_|_|_|_|_|_|_|_|_|_|_|_|_|_|_|_|_|_|_|_|_|_|_|_|_|_|_|_|_|_|_|_|_|_|_|_|

8.   The Wobun-Custis Co.

|_|_|_|_|_|_|_|_|_|_|_|_|_|_|_|_|_|_|_|_|_|_|_|_|_|_|_|_|_|_|_|_|_|_|_|_|

50A Indexing Business and Organization Names With Numbers

Name _____ Date _____

Section _____ Evaluation _____

STUDY THE INDEXING RULE

Some business and organization names contain numbers; for example, *A-1 Bakery* and *17 Clothing Store*. If you look for *17 Clothing Store* in a telephone directory, you will find it under the letter *S*, for *Seventeen Clothing Store*. However, when numbers in a computer file are sorted, they are arranged in order before alphabetic characters. Thus, *17 Clothing Store* would come before *A-1 Bakery* on an alphabetic computer printout. When you create a computer file that contains names with numbers as the first unit, use the following guidelines:

1. If you want numbers to be arranged alphabetically, as they are in a telephone directory, you will have to spell them out when you enter them in your computer file.

2. If you want numbers that are first units to be arranged numerically, they must be lined up at the right. If not, *17 Clothing Store* would come before *8 Brands, Inc.*, because when you sort, the computer will compare the *1* in *17 Clothing Store* with the *8* in *8 Brands, Inc.* Because the *1* comes before *8*, *17* will be listed before *8*. However, if you decide when you create your computer file that you will have numbers with as many as, say, four digits as first units, you can align numbers at the right by inserting one or more zeros before numbers containing fewer than four digits. For example, if you enter *0017* and next *0008*, then the *17* and *8* are aligned at the right. When you sort, the computer will compare the *1* in the *17* with the *zero* before the *8*, and the *17* will be listed *after 8*, which is the correct numeric sequence—*0008*, and next *0017*.

For the exercises in this book, you should index numbers according to guideline *2*, described above; that is, do not spell the numbers out. Instead, align numbers at the right if they are first units. Assume that such numbers will have a maximum of four digits. Study these examples:

LETTERHEAD FORM	INDEXED FORM
1 A Bonding Co.	0001 A BONDING CO
27 Flavors Frozen Yogurt	0027 FLAVORS FROZEN YOGURT
141 Mexican Restaurant	0141 MEXICAN RESTAURANT
The 3010 Professional Building	3010 PROFESSIONAL BUILDING THE
A 1 Video Rentals	A 1 VIDEO RENTALS
Askew's 24-Alley Bowling	ASKEWS 24ALLEY BOWLING
Forty Ports Travel Co.	FORTY PORTS TRAVEL CO*

* Note that if a number is spelled out in letterhead form, you do not change the written form to a numeral but leave it as written.

QUANTUM CORPORATION CLIENT FILE

PRACTICE INDEXING

Write each name in indexed form as shown in the example.

0.   18-Acres Town Houses

| 0 | 0 | 1 | 8 | A | C | R | E | S | | T | O | W | N | | H | O | U | S | E | S | | | | | | | | |

1.   21 Tunes for You, Inc.

2.   186 Clearwater Office Suites

3.   The 1424 Medical Arts Center

4.   B-4 Sundown, Inc.

5.   Burgers by the 100s

6.   Essex 2-4-1 Discounts

7.   Fifty-Fifty Realtors

Name _____ Date _____

Section _____ Evaluation _____

STUDY THE INDEXING RULE

Government names are indexed under the name of the major entity (country, state, county, and city), followed by the distinctive name of the department, bureau, and so on. Federal government names are indexed first under *United States Government* or an abbreviation such as *US Gov*. Using an abbreviation for *United States Government* enables you to do alphabetic sorts with database programs that only sort on the first few characters of a field. It also saves time by enabling your computer to sort faster. For the exercises in this unit, use the abbreviation *US Gov* for the first two units of all federal government names.

LETTERHEAD FORM	INDEXED FORM
Town of Bassett	BASSETT TOWN OF
Bluestone City Schools	BLUESTONE CITY SCHOOLS
Dade County Police	DADE COUNTY POLICE
State of Iowa Corrections Department	IOWA STATE OF CORRECTIONS DEPARTMENT
Louisiana Department of Highways	LOUISIANA HIGHWAYS DEPARTMENT OF
U.S. Department of Defense	US GOV DEFENSE DEPARTMENT OF
Internal Revenue Service	US GOV INTERNAL REVENUE SERVICE
U.S. Labor Department	US GOV LABOR DEPARTMENT

PRACTICE INDEXING

Write each name in indexed form as shown in the example.

0. Port Authority of New York

    |N|E|W| |Y|O|R|K| |P|O|R|T| |A|U|T|H|O|R|I|T|Y| |O|F| | | |

1. City of Orlando

    | | | | | | | | | | | | | | | | | | | | | | | | | | | | | | | | | | | | |

2. Philadelphia Police Department

    | | | | | | | | | | | | | | | | | | | | | | | | | | | | | | | | | | | | |

3. Texas State Department of Health

    | | | | | | | | | | | | | | | | | | | | | | | | | | | | | | | | | | | | |

4. U.S. Department of Agriculture

    | | | | | | | | | | | | | | | | | | | | | | | | | | | | | | | | | | | | |

5.   U.S. Bankruptcy Court

|_|_|_|_|_|_|_|_|_|_|_|_|_|_|_|_|_|_|_|_|_|_|_|_|_|_|_|_|_|_|_|_|_|_|_|_|_|_|_|_

6.   U.S. Department of Justice

|_|_|_|_|_|_|_|_|_|_|_|_|_|_|_|_|_|_|_|_|_|_|_|_|_|_|_|_|_|_|_|_|_|_|_|_|_|_|_|_

7.   U.S. Postal Service

|_|_|_|_|_|_|_|_|_|_|_|_|_|_|_|_|_|_|_|_|_|_|_|_|_|_|_|_|_|_|_|_|_|_|_|_|_|_|_|_

8.   State of Utah Compensation Board

|_|_|_|_|_|_|_|_|_|_|_|_|_|_|_|_|_|_|_|_|_|_|_|_|_|_|_|_|_|_|_|_|_|_|_|_|_|_|_|_

Name _____   Date _____

Section _____   Evaluation _____

In this exercise you will enter the indexed client names on the 56 client account forms. Follow these steps.

a.   Turn to page 89 and find Quantum Corporation's client account form number 001. The form numbers are in the upper right corner and are only for reference in this book.

b.   Note that the name of the client is *7 Seas Publishing Co., Inc.* The name is keyed in letterhead form.

c.   Note that there are spaces for the indexed name that have not been filled in. Write the name in indexed form in these spaces. Write one letter or number in each space. Write three zeros before the *7* (0007) so that numbers that are first units will align at the right. Leave a blank space between units. The "Indexed Name" section of form 001 should look like this when you are finished. Note that a handwritten *0* (zero) has a diagonal line across it so that it will not look like the letter *O*.

Indexed
Name |0|0|0|7| |S|E|A|S| |P|U|B|L|I|S|H|I|N|G| |C|O| |I|N|C| |

d.   Follow Step C for forms 002 through 056. Your instructor may ask you to check your work against the key on page 149. If so, check each entry carefully and make corrections if necessary.

Creating the Client File

Name _____ Date _____

Section _____ Evaluation _____

Note: Your instructor may tell you to skip this exercise if you are using the data diskette.

In this exercise you are to create a computer file that will contain the data on forms 001 through 056. The contents of the **LNAME** field come from the Quantum employee file in Unit II. The last name of the client's representative is entered in this field. Each of the seven client representatives was assigned clients according to their organization type. Two of the client representatives were assigned clients by geographic location.

Field information for the client file is given below:

FIELD CONTENTS	FIELD NAME	LENGTH	TYPE
Account Number	ACCTNO	5	Numeric
Name	NAME	38	Character
Client Representative	LNAME	12	Character
Indexed Name	INAME	38	Character
Address	ADDRESS	35	Character
City	CITY	20	Character
State	STATE	2	Character
ZIP Code	ZIP	10	Character
Phone Number	PHONE	12	Character
No. of Employees	EMPNUM	4	Numeric
Major Product/Service	PS	30	Character
Organization Type	OTYPE	1	Character

Note: The name of the Client Representative field is called **LNAME.** It is essential to use **LNAME** because the last name of the client representative in the employee file is also named **LNAME.** In order to share information from both files, the field in common must be defined with the same **name, type,** and **length.**

QUANTUM CORPORATION
CLIENT FILE

Creating a Custom Screen

Name _____ Date _____

Section _____ Evaluation _____

Note: Your instructor may tell you to skip this exercise if you are using the data diskette.

If your database program allows the development of a custom screen, design a screen that closely resembles the source document. Also, build in protection so that data will be entered in the correct format. For example, if you want the state to be entered in all capital letters, build that feature into the screen. If this is done, the state will be entered into the file in uppercase letters regardless of the manner in which it is keyed. Also, if you have the ability to print instructions for the user of the file, you should do so. Your instructor may provide this screen design for you, or you may be asked to develop your own.

Inputting Data From Forms 001 Through 024

Name _____ Date _____

Section _____ Evaluation _____

Note: Your instructor may tell you to skip this exercise if you are using the data diskette.

You should have two disks formatted before you begin to enter data. You will save your data on one of these disks, and the other will be used for a backup.

In this exercise, you will begin to enter the data from the client account forms into the database. Remove forms 001 through 024, pages 89 through 94. Key the data on each form, field by field.

After you complete the entries for each form, be sure to check your work. By correcting errors before going to the next form, you will save yourself a great deal of trouble later.

EXERCISE 54

Inputting Data From Forms 025 Through 056

Name _____ Date _____

Section _____ Evaluation _____

Note: Your instructor may tell you to skip this exercise if you are using the data diskette.

Enter the data from each form as you did in Exercise 53.

EXERCISE 55

Listing the Entire Client File

Name _____ Date _____

Section _____ Evaluation _____

Make a listing of the client file of Quantum Corporation.

Your listing should be in alphabetic order by the Indexed Name field (not the Name field). Use as few sheets as possible for your printout.

After you have completed your listing, carefully proofread for errors. You have already checked each screen (record) of information as you entered it, but accuracy is so important that you must take the time now to check your work again. Any errors will affect the information you get from your file. If you find any errors, make the corrections now. Turn to page 150 in the back of this book and check your work against the key to make sure that your list is in proper alphabetic order by indexed name.

Answering Client Inquiries

Name _____   Date _____

Section _____   Evaluation _____

One of the fields in the Quantum client file is the Organization Type field. Each client is classified in the field according to one of six single-letter codes as shown in this table:

CODE	ORGANIZATION TYPE
g	government
m	manufacturing
n	nonprofit
r	retail
s	service
w	wholesale

Another field in the file is the Major Product-Service field. Listed here is an alphabetic index of the terms used in that field.

MAJOR PRODUCT-SERVICE INDEX

auto rentals
automotive
bakery
ball bearings
bank
clothing
computer components
computers
cosmetics
court of law
dairy products
day care
department store
disaster relief
educational research
  (ed. research)
electronic components
  (elec. components)
emergency telephone service
  (emerg. tele. serv.)
financial advice
food and shelter—indigents
  (food and shelter)
funeral home
gasoline
gifts
ground tranportation
guard service
hardware
health spa
hotels

investments
laundry
lumber
medical research
mining
music
novelties
paper products
postal service
prescription drugs
public recreation area
  (public rec. area)
publishing
radio station
restaurant
school
service club
sporting goods
tanning salon
tax collection
tax preparation
television
textiles
transportation
travel
trucking
vehicle registration
video rentals
waterbeds—furniture
word processing
word processors

QUANTUM CORPORATION
CLIENT FILE

Use the information in the Organization Type code table and the Major Product-Service Index to help you in searching for the following information in the file.

a. One of the clients is considering developing a new product for use by retailers. Find how many retail stores are on file so that the client will know whether or not a survey would be feasible. How many? _____

b. A client wants to contact all of the client travel agencies in California. What are their names and telephone numbers? _____

_____

_____

c. How many manufacturers are on file who employ more than 750 workers? _____

d. A client requests the complete company name and address for 3 M Supply. What is it?

Name _____

Address _____

City _____ State _____ ZIP _____

e. How many retailers are on file who sell clothing? (Be sure to include department and sporting goods stores, as well as clothing stores.) _____

Finding the Number of Clients by Organization Type

Name _____ Date _____

Section _____ Evaluation _____

The administrative assistant in the research department wants to know how many clients are on file by organization type.

a. Total number of manufacturing, retail, service, and wholesale businesses:

_____

What is the percentage of the total? _____

b. Number of nonprofit organizations? _____

c. Number of government agencies? _____

Adding New Clients

Name _____ Date _____

Section _____ Evaluation _____

You have received client account records for new clients. Remove forms 057 through 060 on page 103 (Be sure to save forms 061 through 064 for Exercise 59.), and add these clients to the file.

QUANTUM CORPORATION CLIENT FILE

EXERCISE
59
Updating Client Records

Name _____ Date _____

Section _____ Evaluation _____

Remove forms 061 through 064 on page 104, and update the client records as indicated.

EXERCISE
60
Preparing Mailing Labels for Wholesalers

Name _____ Date _____

Section _____ Evaluation _____

Prepare mailing labels for a survey to be sent to all wholesalers. Be sure to print the Name field, *not* the Indexed Name field. The mailing labels should be arranged by ZIP Code.

EXERCISE
61
Finding the Researchers

Name _____ Date _____

Section _____ Evaluation _____

Print a list of all companies that do any kind of research. Be sure to print the names from the Name field, but index on the Indexed Name field. *Hint:* Study the Major Product-Service Index on page 79 and find all occurrences of the term *research*.

82

Searching for Product-Service Categories

Name _____ Date _____

Section _____ Evaluation _____

Paula Woo has sent you a memo asking for the following information. She will call you about it later, so write it down now and have it ready.

Hint: Refer to the Major Product-Service field for these searches.

a. Number of day-care organizations on file? _____

b. Number of restaurants on file? _____

c. Number of radio stations on file? _____

d. Number of lumber companies on file? _____

Searching for Clients in Los Angeles and Their Client Representatives

Name _____ Date _____

Section _____ Evaluation _____

Because the employee file and client file have the Name field, **LNAME,** in common, information can be obtained from both files while working in either file. For this search, list each client in Los Angeles, the client representative, and the client representative's phone number.

Because the client representative's phone number is in the employee file, you will use special commands to perform this search. If your database program does not allow you to relate data in one file to another, omit this exercise.

EXERCISE 64
Reporting the Total Number of Clients Served by Each Client Representative

Name _____ Date _____

Section _____ Evaluation _____

Create a summary report listing the total number of clients serviced by each client representative. Report the client representatives in alphabetic order.

EXERCISE 65
Deleting Client Records

Name _____ Date _____

Section _____ Evaluation _____

You have been sent four client account records containing deletions. Remove forms 065 through 068 on page 105 (Be sure to save forms 069 through 072 for Exercise 69.), and delete these records from the file.

EXERCISE 66
Listing Washington State Retailers

Name _____ Date _____

Section _____ Evaluation _____

You have been asked to supply the sales department with a list of all retailers in the state of Washington. Print a listing indexed by the Account Number field, including the account number, name, ZIP code, and number of employees for each record.

How many retailers in the state of Washington? _____

EXERCISE 67

Listing the San Francisco Clients

Name _____   Date _____

Section _____   Evaluation _____

You have been asked to furnish a list of the San Francisco clients for a market survey. Print a listing indexed by the Account Number field, including the account number, the name of the client, the client representative, and the client representative's phone number.

How many San Francisco clients? _____

Note: You will need to establish a relationship between the two files as you did in Exercise 63.

EXERCISE 68

Listing the Government Agencies

Name _____   Date _____

Section _____   Evaluation _____

List the government agencies indexed according to the City field; include in the listing the city, state, agency name, and account number.

How many government agencies? _____

EXERCISE
69
Updating Client Records

Name _____ Date _____

Section _____ Evaluation _____

More updates have just come in. Remove forms 069 through 072 on page 106, and make the indicated changes.

EXERCISE
70
Adding More New Clients

Name _____ Date _____

Section _____ Evaluation _____

You have received four new companies to add to the file. Remove forms 073 through 076 on page 107 (Be sure to save forms 077 through 080 for Exercise 75B), and add the new clients to the file.

EXERCISE
71
Creating Mailing Labels for Selected Clients

Name _____ Date _____

Section _____ Evaluation _____

Quantum Corporation is planning to survey all clients with at least 2500 employees other than government agencies and nonprofit organizations. Print mailing labels for these businesses, arranged by ZIP code.

How many labels? _____

86

Listing the Service Businesses in California

Name _____ Date _____

Section _____ Evaluation _____

Create a listing of all the service businesses in California for the research director to use in a special project. Index the listing by city, and include the following fields: City, Name of Business, and Major Product-Service.

How many service businesses in California? _____

Preparing for Small - Organization Survey

Name _____ Date _____

Section _____ Evaluation _____

The company is preparing to survey all clients with fewer than 25 employees. Print a list showing the names of the organizations and the number of employees. The list should be indexed by Indexed Name field, but the Name field should be used for the printout.

How many small organizations? _____

EXERCISE 74

Finding the Companies

Name _____   Date _____

Section _____   Evaluation _____

Which manufacturing businesses produce ball bearings?

_____

_____

EXERCISE 75A

Test – Quantum Corporation, Client File

Your instructor will give you the test for this unit.

EXERCISE 75B

Optional Exercises in Indexing and Data Entry

Name _____   Date _____

Section _____   Evaluation _____

Index the names on forms 077 through 104. Check your work against the key on page 150. After making the needed corrections, if any, enter the records into your client file.

CLIENT ACCOUNT FORM 001

Quantum Corporation

[X] ADD   [ ] MODIFY   [ ] DELETE

ACCOUNT NUMBER	NAME	REPRESENTATIVE (Last Name)
00009	7 Seas Publishing Co.	Lyle

INDEXED NAME

ADDRESS	CITY	STATE	ZIP
2003 South Harbor Boulevard	Anaheim	CA	92805

PHONE	NO. OF EMPLOYEES	MAJOR PRODUCT/SERVICE	ORGANIZATION TYPE
213-555-2888	1200	publishing	r

CLIENT ACCOUNT FORM 002

Quantum Corporation

[X] ADD   [ ] MODIFY   [ ] DELETE

ACCOUNT NUMBER	NAME	REPRESENTATIVE (Last Name)
00010	Word Technology, Inc.Inc.	Lyle

INDEXED NAME

ADDRESS	CITY	STATE	ZIP
309 Third Street South	Anaheim	CA	91801

PHONE	NO. OF EMPLOYEES	MAJOR PRODUCT/SERVICE	ORGANIZATION TYPE
213-555-2323	260	word processors	r

CLIENT ACCOUNT FORM 003

Quantum Corporation

[X] ADD   [ ] MODIFY   [ ] DELETE

ACCOUNT NUMBER	NAME	REPRESENTATIVE (Last Name)
00030	The 76 Trombones Music Store	Lyle

INDEXED NAME

ADDRESS	CITY	STATE	ZIP
717 Normandie Avenue	Los Angeles	CA	90005

PHONE	NO. OF EMPLOYEES	MAJOR PRODUCT/SERVICE	ORGANIZATION TYPE
213-555-8923	450	music	r

CLIENT ACCOUNT FORM 004

Quantum Corporation

[X] ADD   [ ] MODIFY   [ ] DELETE

ACCOUNT NUMBER	NAME	REPRESENTATIVE (Last Name)
00032	Tropez Tanning Salon	Price

INDEXED NAME

ADDRESS	CITY	STATE	ZIP
200 South Broadway	Los Angeles	CA	90013

PHONE	NO. OF EMPLOYEES	MAJOR PRODUCT/SERVICE	ORGANIZATION TYPE
213-555-5656	40	tanning salon	s

CLIENT ACCOUNT FORM

Quantum Corporation

[X] ADD [ ] MODIFY [ ] DELETE

005

ACCOUNT NUMBER	NAME	REPRESENTATIVE (Last Name)
00044	Travelers' Inns, Inc.	Price

INDEXED NAME

ADDRESS	CITY	STATE	ZIP
3190 West 7th Street	Los Angeles	CA	90005

PHONE	NO. OF EMPLOYEES	MAJOR PRODUCT/SERVICE	ORGANIZATION TYPE
213-555-8922	1800	hotel	s

CLIENT ACCOUNT FORM

Quantum Corporation

[X] ADD [ ] MODIFY [ ] DELETE

006

ACCOUNT NUMBER	NAME	REPRESENTATIVE (Last Name)
00051	Suzzette's School	Price

INDEXED NAME

ADDRESS	CITY	STATE	ZIP
700 Hollywood Boulevard	Los Angeles	CA	90046

PHONE	NO. OF EMPLOYEES	MAJOR PRODUCT/SERVICE	ORGANIZATION TYPE
213-555-4572	100	school	s

CLIENT ACCOUNT FORM

Quantum Corporation

[X] ADD [ ] MODIFY [ ] DELETE

007

ACCOUNT NUMBER	NAME	REPRESENTATIVE (Last Name)
00059	10 20 Automotive Supply Co.	Lyle

INDEXED NAME

ADDRESS	CITY	STATE	ZIP
10330 Wilshire Boulevard	Los Angeles	CA	90024

PHONE	NO. OF EMPLOYEES	MAJOR PRODUCT/SERVICE	ORGANIZATION TYPE
213-555-6862	800	automotive	r

CLIENT ACCOUNT FORM

Quantum Corporation

[X] ADD [ ] MODIFY [ ] DELETE

008

ACCOUNT NUMBER	NAME	REPRESENTATIVE (Last Name)
00062	Wordex Corp.	Price

INDEXED NAME

ADDRESS	CITY	STATE	ZIP
500 South Flower	Los Angeles	CA	90071

PHONE	NO. OF EMPLOYEES	MAJOR PRODUCT/SERVICE	ORGANIZATION TYPE
213-555-3490	150	word processing	s

CLIENT ACCOUNT FORM 009

Quantum Corporation

[X] ADD   [ ] MODIFY   [ ] DELETE

ACCOUNT NUMBER	NAME	REPRESENTATIVE (Last Name)
00066	Silverton Electronics	Treat

INDEXED NAME

ADDRESS	CITY	STATE	ZIP
10600 Wilshire Boulevard	Los Angeles	CA	90024

PHONE	NO. OF EMPLOYEES	MAJOR PRODUCT/SERVICE	ORGANIZATION TYPE
213-555-3348	350	computer components	m

CLIENT ACCOUNT FORM 010

Quantum Corporation

[X] ADD   [ ] MODIFY   [ ] DELETE

ACCOUNT NUMBER	NAME	REPRESENTATIVE (Last Name)
00068	WRG FM 96	Price

INDEXED NAME

ADDRESS	CITY	STATE	ZIP
107 West 3d	Los Angeles	CA	90013

PHONE	NO. OF EMPLOYEES	MAJOR PRODUCT/SERVICE	ORGANIZATION TYPE
213-555-7878	25	radio station	s

CLIENT ACCOUNT FORM 011

Quantum Corporation

[X] ADD   [ ] MODIFY   [ ] DELETE

ACCOUNT NUMBER	NAME	REPRESENTATIVE (Last Name)
00070	U.S. Department of Interior	Treat

INDEXED NAME

ADDRESS	CITY	STATE	ZIP
800 North Broadway	Los Angeles	CA	90012

PHONE	NO. OF EMPLOYEES	MAJOR PRODUCT/SERVICE	ORGANIZATION TYPE
213-555-5482	85	public rec. area	g

CLIENT ACCOUNT FORM 012

Quantum Corporation

[X] ADD   [ ] MODIFY   [ ] DELETE

ACCOUNT NUMBER	NAME	REPRESENTATIVE (Last Name)
00075	U.S. Department of Education	Treat

INDEXED NAME

ADDRESS	CITY	STATE	ZIP
225 Temple	Los Angeles	CA	90012

PHONE	NO. OF EMPLOYEES	MAJOR PRODUCT/SERVICE	ORGANIZATION TYPE
213-555-2352	120	ed. research	g

CLIENT ACCOUNT FORM — 013

Quantum Corporation

[X] ADD [ ] MODIFY [ ] DELETE

ACCOUNT NUMBER	NAME	REPRESENTATIVE (Last Name)
00088	6001 Pearson Place Clothing Outlets	Eberhard

INDEXED NAME

ADDRESS	CITY	STATE	ZIP
412 Montgomery	San Francisco	CA	94104

PHONE	NO. OF EMPLOYEES	MAJOR PRODUCT/SERVICE	ORGANIZATION TYPE
415-555-2525	400	clothing	w

CLIENT ACCOUNT FORM — 014

Quantum Corporation

[X] ADD [ ] MODIFY [ ] DELETE

ACCOUNT NUMBER	NAME	REPRESENTATIVE (Last Name)
00089	Value Plus Drug Stores	Lyle

INDEXED NAME

ADDRESS	CITY	STATE	ZIP
124 Alameda South	Los Angeles	CA	90012

PHONE	NO. OF EMPLOYEES	MAJOR PRODUCT/SERVICE	ORGANIZATION TYPE
213-555-7825	1200	prescription drugs	r

CLIENT ACCOUNT FORM — 015

Quantum Corporation

[X] ADD [ ] MODIFY [ ] DELETE

ACCOUNT NUMBER	NAME	REPRESENTATIVE (Last Name)
00090	2001 Technologies, Inc.	Treat

INDEXED NAME

ADDRESS	CITY	STATE	ZIP
404 West Washington Boulevard	Los Angeles	CA	90015

PHONE	NO. OF EMPLOYEES	MAJOR PRODUCT/SERVICE	ORGANIZATION TYPE
213-555-5672	650	computer components	m

CLIENT ACCOUNT FORM — 016

Quantum Corporation

[X] ADD [ ] MODIFY [ ] DELETE

ACCOUNT NUMBER	NAME	REPRESENTATIVE (Last Name)
00095	Varner Research Center	Holmes

INDEXED NAME

ADDRESS	CITY	STATE	ZIP
1129 South Hill	Los Angeles	CA	90015

PHONE	NO. OF EMPLOYEES	MAJOR PRODUCT/SERVICE	ORGANIZATION TYPE
213-555-9242	250	medical research	n

CLIENT ACCOUNT FORM

Quantum Corporation

017

[X] ADD ☐ MODIFY ☐ DELETE

ACCOUNT NUMBER	NAME	REPRESENTATIVE (Last Name)
00102	S and T Hardware	Lyle

INDEXED NAME

ADDRESS	CITY	STATE	ZIP
1700 West Clinton Avenue	Fresno	CA	93705

PHONE	NO. OF EMPLOYEES	MAJOR PRODUCT/SERVICE	ORGANIZATION TYPE
209-555-7844	20	hardware	r

CLIENT ACCOUNT FORM

Quantum Corporation

018

[X] ADD ☐ MODIFY ☐ DELETE

ACCOUNT NUMBER	NAME	REPRESENTATIVE (Last Name)
00110	Wordesign, Inc.	Lyle

INDEXED NAME

ADDRESS	CITY	STATE	ZIP
633 East Belmont Avenue	Fresno	CA	93728

PHONE	NO. OF EMPLOYEES	MAJOR PRODUCT/SERVICE	ORGANIZATION TYPE
209-555-3232	60	word processors	r

CLIENT ACCOUNT FORM

Quantum Corporation

019

[X] ADD ☐ MODIFY ☐ DELETE

ACCOUNT NUMBER	NAME	REPRESENTATIVE (Last Name)
00112	Van Tech, Inc.	Sharpe

INDEXED NAME

ADDRESS	CITY	STATE	ZIP
333 North Parkway Drive	Seattle	WA	98109

PHONE	NO. OF EMPLOYEES	MAJOR PRODUCT/SERVICE	ORGANIZATION TYPE
206-555-7372	2500	elec. components	m

CLIENT ACCOUNT FORM

Quantum Corporation

020

[X] ADD ☐ MODIFY ☐ DELETE

ACCOUNT NUMBER	NAME	REPRESENTATIVE (Last Name)
00130	VIP Sales	Eberhard

INDEXED NAME

ADDRESS	CITY	STATE	ZIP
217 Capitol Street	Sacramento	CA	95814

PHONE	NO. OF EMPLOYEES	MAJOR PRODUCT/SERVICE	ORGANIZATION TYPE
916-555-9023	240	automotive	w

Quantum Corporation — CLIENT ACCOUNT FORM — 021

[X] ADD [ ] MODIFY [ ] DELETE

ACCOUNT NUMBER	NAME	REPRESENTATIVE (Last Name)
00138	R and R Travel Service, Inc.	Price

INDEXED NAME: | | | | | | | | | | | | | | | | | | | | | | | |

ADDRESS	CITY	STATE	ZIP
1020 2d Avenue	San Diego	CA	92102

PHONE	NO. OF EMPLOYEES	MAJOR PRODUCT/SERVICE	ORGANIZATION TYPE
619-555-2592	55	travel	s

Quantum Corporation — CLIENT ACCOUNT FORM — 022

[X] ADD [ ] MODIFY [ ] DELETE

ACCOUNT NUMBER	NAME	REPRESENTATIVE (Last Name)
00140	Y. H. Wilder and Sons	Sharpe

INDEXED NAME: | | | | | | | | | | | | | | | | | | | | | | | |

ADDRESS	CITY	STATE	ZIP
3400 Kenyon	Seattle	WA	98101

PHONE	NO. OF EMPLOYEES	MAJOR PRODUCT/SERVICE	ORGANIZATION TYPE
206-555-4067	70	clothing	r

Quantum Corporation — CLIENT ACCOUNT FORM — 023

[X] ADD [ ] MODIFY [ ] DELETE

ACCOUNT NUMBER	NAME	REPRESENTATIVE (Last Name)
00161	2 A Novelties	Eberhard

INDEXED NAME: | | | | | | | | | | | | | | | | | | | | | | | |

ADDRESS	CITY	STATE	ZIP
1130 Grand Avenue	Los Angeles	CA	90015

PHONE	NO. OF EMPLOYEES	MAJOR PRODUCT/SERVICE	ORGANIZATION TYPE
213-555-3892	280	novelties	w

Quantum Corporation — CLIENT ACCOUNT FORM — 024

[X] ADD [ ] MODIFY [ ] DELETE

ACCOUNT NUMBER	NAME	REPRESENTATIVE (Last Name)
00166	Trust Help Line	Holmes

INDEXED NAME: | | | | | | | | | | | | | | | | | | | | | | | |

ADDRESS	CITY	STATE	ZIP
450 Golden Gate Avenue	San Francisco	CA	94102

PHONE	NO. OF EMPLOYEES	MAJOR PRODUCT/SERVICE	ORGANIZATION TYPE
415-555-7872	15	emerg. tele. serv.	n

CLIENT ACCOUNT FORM 025

Quantum Corporation

[X] ADD [ ] MODIFY [ ] DELETE

ACCOUNT NUMBER	NAME	REPRESENTATIVE (Last Name)
00167	3 M Supply Co.	Eberhard

INDEXED NAME

ADDRESS	CITY	STATE	ZIP
3030 Geary Boulevard	San Francisco	CA	94118

PHONE	NO. OF EMPLOYEES	MAJOR PRODUCT/SERVICE	ORGANIZATION TYPE
415-555-9823	465	paper products	w

CLIENT ACCOUNT FORM 026

Quantum Corporation

[X] ADD [ ] MODIFY [ ] DELETE

ACCOUNT NUMBER	NAME	REPRESENTATIVE (Last Name)
00169	Travelers Help	Price

INDEXED NAME

ADDRESS	CITY	STATE	ZIP
105 4th Street	San Francisco	CA	94103

PHONE	NO. OF EMPLOYEES	MAJOR PRODUCT/SERVICE	ORGANIZATION TYPE
415-555-7823	35	travel	s

CLIENT ACCOUNT FORM 027

Quantum Corporation

[X] ADD [ ] MODIFY [ ] DELETE

ACCOUNT NUMBER	NAME	REPRESENTATIVE (Last Name)
00177	U. S. Postal Service	Treat

INDEXED NAME

ADDRESS	CITY	STATE	ZIP
99 7th Street	San Francisco	CA	94103

PHONE	NO. OF EMPLOYEES	MAJOR PRODUCT/SERVICE	ORGANIZATION TYPE
415-555-2121	285	postal service	g

CLIENT ACCOUNT FORM 028

Quantum Corporation

[X] ADD [ ] MODIFY [ ] DELETE

ACCOUNT NUMBER	NAME	REPRESENTATIVE (Last Name)
00180	War Against Cancer	Holmes

INDEXED NAME

ADDRESS	CITY	STATE	ZIP
244 Sansome Avenue	San Francisco	CA	94120

PHONE	NO. OF EMPLOYEES	MAJOR PRODUCT/SERVICE	ORGANIZATION TYPE
415-555-9832	345	medical research	n

CLIENT ACCOUNT FORM

Quantum Corporation — 029

☒ ADD ☐ MODIFY ☐ DELETE

ACCOUNT NUMBER	NAME	REPRESENTATIVE (Last Name)
00183	Target MS	Holmes

INDEXED NAME

ADDRESS	CITY	STATE	ZIP
430 Stockton Boulevard	San Francisco	CA	94106

PHONE	NO. OF EMPLOYEES	MAJOR PRODUCT/SERVICE	ORGANIZATION TYPE
415-555-6863	780	medical research	n

CLIENT ACCOUNT FORM

Quantum Corporation — 030

☒ ADD ☐ MODIFY ☐ DELETE

ACCOUNT NUMBER	NAME	REPRESENTATIVE (Last Name)
00190	Wake Co Manufacturing	Treat

INDEXED NAME

ADDRESS	CITY	STATE	ZIP
Geary Inds. Pk. 486 Geary	San Francisco	CA	94101

PHONE	NO. OF EMPLOYEES	MAJOR PRODUCT/SERVICE	ORGANIZATION TYPE
415-555-9420	590	ball bearings	m

CLIENT ACCOUNT FORM

Quantum Corporation — 031

☒ ADD ☐ MODIFY ☐ DELETE

ACCOUNT NUMBER	NAME	REPRESENTATIVE (Last Name)
00204	Saxton Distributors	Eberhard

INDEXED NAME

ADDRESS	CITY	STATE	ZIP
250 Taylor Street	San Francisco	CA	94102

PHONE	NO. OF EMPLOYEES	MAJOR PRODUCT/SERVICE	ORGANIZATION TYPE
415-555-2027	285	novelties	w

CLIENT ACCOUNT FORM

Quantum Corporation — 032

☒ ADD ☐ MODIFY ☐ DELETE

ACCOUNT NUMBER	NAME	REPRESENTATIVE (Last Name)
00225	3 Way Department Stores	Lyle

INDEXED NAME

ADDRESS	CITY	STATE	ZIP
300 West Broadway	Bakersfield	CA	93310

PHONE	NO. OF EMPLOYEES	MAJOR PRODUCT/SERVICE	ORGANIZATION TYPE
707-555-9293	865	department stores	r

CLIENT ACCOUNT FORM

Quantum Corporation

033

[X] ADD   [ ] MODIFY   [ ] DELETE

ACCOUNT NUMBER	NAME	REPRESENTATIVE (Last Name)
00231	Uncle Pete's Place	Nelson

INDEXED NAME

ADDRESS	CITY	STATE	ZIP
1000 West 22d Avenue	Portland	OR	97210

PHONE	NO. OF EMPLOYEES	MAJOR PRODUCT/SERVICE	ORGANIZATION TYPE
503-555-2025	20	restaurant	s

CLIENT ACCOUNT FORM

Quantum Corporation

034

[X] ADD   [ ] MODIFY   [ ] DELETE

ACCOUNT NUMBER	NAME	REPRESENTATIVE (Last Name)
00242	Thurston Enterprises	Nelson

INDEXED NAME

ADDRESS	CITY	STATE	ZIP
725 SW Alder	Portland	OR	97205

PHONE	NO. OF EMPLOYEES	MAJOR PRODUCT/SERVICE	ORGANIZATION TYPE
503-555-9323	2780	ball bearings	m

CLIENT ACCOUNT FORM

Quantum Corporation

035

[X] ADD   [ ] MODIFY   [ ] DELETE

ACCOUNT NUMBER	NAME	REPRESENTATIVE (Last Name)
00247	Serv n Go Drive In's	Nelson

INDEXED NAME

ADDRESS	CITY	STATE	ZIP
440 Lincoln	Spokane	WA	99201

PHONE	NO. OF EMPLOYEES	MAJOR PRODUCT/SERVICE	ORGANIZATION TYPE
509-555-4505	765	restaurant	s

CLIENT ACCOUNT FORM

Quantum Corporation

036

[X] ADD   [ ] MODIFY   [ ] DELETE

ACCOUNT NUMBER	NAME	REPRESENTATIVE (Last Name)
00255	Internal Revenue Service	Nelson

INDEXED NAME

ADDRESS	CITY	STATE	ZIP
319 SW Pine	Portland	OR	97204

PHONE	NO. OF EMPLOYEES	MAJOR PRODUCT/SERVICE	ORGANIZATION TYPE
503-555-4599	25	tax collection	g

CLIENT ACCOUNT FORM 037

Quantum Corporation

- [X] ADD
- [ ] MODIFY
- [ ] DELETE

ACCOUNT NUMBER	NAME	REPRESENTATIVE (Last Name)
00262	Tour America Bus Lines	Nelson

INDEXED NAME

ADDRESS	CITY	STATE	ZIP
170 West Main Street	Portland	OR	97201

PHONE	NO. OF EMPLOYEES	MAJOR PRODUCT/SERVICE	ORGANIZATION TYPE
503-555-0235	180	transportation	s

CLIENT ACCOUNT FORM 038

Quantum Corporation

- [X] ADD
- [ ] MODIFY
- [ ] DELETE

ACCOUNT NUMBER	NAME	REPRESENTATIVE (Last Name)
00275	S and N Stores, Inc.	Nelson

INDEXED NAME

ADDRESS	CITY	STATE	ZIP
240 West Trent Avenue	Spokane	WA	99201

PHONE	NO. OF EMPLOYEES	MAJOR PRODUCT/SERVICE	ORGANIZATION TYPE
509-555-2620	85	sporting goods	r

CLIENT ACCOUNT FORM 039

Quantum Corporation

- [X] ADD
- [ ] MODIFY
- [ ] DELETE

ACCOUNT NUMBER	NAME	REPRESENTATIVE (Last Name)
00283	R. T. Stanley Manufacturers	Nelson

INDEXED NAME

ADDRESS	CITY	STATE	ZIP
2020 Riverside	Spokane	WA	99201

PHONE	NO. OF EMPLOYEES	MAJOR PRODUCT/SERVICE	ORGANIZATION TYPE
509-555-5209	2500	textiles	m

CLIENT ACCOUNT FORM 040

Quantum Corporation

- [X] ADD
- [ ] MODIFY
- [ ] DELETE

ACCOUNT NUMBER	NAME	REPRESENTATIVE (Last Name)
00292	Wesley Distributors	Nelson

INDEXED NAME

ADDRESS	CITY	STATE	ZIP
700 North Howard Street	Spokane	WA	97201

PHONE	NO. OF EMPLOYEES	MAJOR PRODUCT/SERVICE	ORGANIZATION TYPE
509-555-0341	930	clothing	w

CLIENT ACCOUNT FORM

Quantum Corporation

041

[X] ADD [ ] MODIFY [ ] DELETE

ACCOUNT NUMBER	NAME	REPRESENTATIVE (Last Name)
00300	WXTP AM FM	Nelson

INDEXED NAME

ADDRESS	CITY	STATE	ZIP
510 West 6th Avenue	Spokane	WA	99204

PHONE	NO. OF EMPLOYEES	MAJOR PRODUCT/SERVICE	ORGANIZATION TYPE
509-555-4503	65	radio station	s

CLIENT ACCOUNT FORM

Quantum Corporation

042

[X] ADD [ ] MODIFY [ ] DELETE

ACCOUNT NUMBER	NAME	REPRESENTATIVE (Last Name)
00304	Silverton Mining Co.	Nelson

INDEXED NAME

ADDRESS	CITY	STATE	ZIP
Route 3	Startup	WA	98293

PHONE	NO. OF EMPLOYEES	MAJOR PRODUCT/SERVICE	ORGANIZATION TYPE
509-555-2822	900	mining	m

CLIENT ACCOUNT FORM

Quantum Corporation

043

[X] ADD [ ] MODIFY [ ] DELETE

ACCOUNT NUMBER	NAME	REPRESENTATIVE (Last Name)
00420	W. B. Walker and Sons, Inc.	Sharpe

INDEXED NAME

ADDRESS	CITY	STATE	ZIP
17600 Pacific Highway	Seattle	WA	98188

PHONE	NO. OF EMPLOYEES	MAJOR PRODUCT/SERVICE	ORGANIZATION TYPE
206-555-8984	530	textiles	m

CLIENT ACCOUNT FORM

Quantum Corporation

044

[X] ADD [ ] MODIFY [ ] DELETE

ACCOUNT NUMBER	NAME	REPRESENTATIVE (Last Name)
00429	Williams Warehouses, Inc.	Sharpe

INDEXED NAME

ADDRESS	CITY	STATE	ZIP
2820 North Pacific Highway	Seattle	WA	98195

PHONE	NO. OF EMPLOYEES	MAJOR PRODUCT/SERVICE	ORGANIZATION TYPE
206-555-3830	485	clothing	w

CLIENT ACCOUNT FORM

Quantum Corporation

045

[X] ADD [ ] MODIFY [ ] DELETE

ACCOUNT NUMBER	NAME	REPRESENTATIVE (Last Name)
00440	Vivian's Sundries, Inc.	Eberhard

INDEXED NAME

ADDRESS	CITY	STATE	ZIP
1000 9th Avenue NW	San Diego	CA	92110

PHONE	NO. OF EMPLOYEES	MAJOR PRODUCT/SERVICE	ORGANIZATION TYPE
619-555-7620	430	novelties	w

CLIENT ACCOUNT FORM

Quantum Corporation

046

[X] ADD [ ] MODIFY [ ] DELETE

ACCOUNT NUMBER	NAME	REPRESENTATIVE (Last Name)
00465	S'Mores Bakery, Inc.	Sharpe

INDEXED NAME

ADDRESS	CITY	STATE	ZIP
4445 Beacon Avenue South	Seattle	WA	98108

PHONE	NO. OF EMPLOYEES	MAJOR PRODUCT/SERVICE	ORGANIZATION TYPE
206-555-9101	245	bakery	m

CLIENT ACCOUNT FORM

Quantum Corporation

047

[X] ADD [ ] MODIFY [ ] DELETE

ACCOUNT NUMBER	NAME	REPRESENTATIVE (Last Name)
00472	3 Hour Laundry	Sharpe

INDEXED NAME

ADDRESS	CITY	STATE	ZIP
900 Western Way	Seattle	WA	98104

PHONE	NO. OF EMPLOYEES	MAJOR PRODUCT/SERVICE	ORGANIZATION TYPE
206-555-4842	85	laundry	s

CLIENT ACCOUNT FORM

Quantum Corporation

048

[X] ADD [ ] MODIFY [ ] DELETE

ACCOUNT NUMBER	NAME	REPRESENTATIVE (Last Name)
00488	The Safe Way	Sharpe

INDEXED NAME

ADDRESS	CITY	STATE	ZIP
1012 Columbia	Seattle	WA	98104

PHONE	NO. OF EMPLOYEES	MAJOR PRODUCT/SERVICE	ORGANIZATION TYPE
206-555-4249	165	guards	s

CLIENT ACCOUNT FORM 049

Quantum Corporation

[X] ADD [ ] MODIFY [ ] DELETE

ACCOUNT NUMBER	NAME	REPRESENTATIVE (Last Name)
00490	Techni Comp	Sharpe

INDEXED NAME

ADDRESS	CITY	STATE	ZIP
500 Stewart Circle	Seattle	WA	98101

PHONE	NO. OF EMPLOYEES	MAJOR PRODUCT/SERVICE	ORGANIZATION TYPE
206-555-2429	45	computers	r

CLIENT ACCOUNT FORM 050

Quantum Corporation

[X] ADD [ ] MODIFY [ ] DELETE

ACCOUNT NUMBER	NAME	REPRESENTATIVE (Last Name)
00500	The Rest Shop Restaurant	Sharpe

INDEXED NAME

ADDRESS	CITY	STATE	ZIP
2849 Pacific	Seattle	WA	98195

PHONE	NO. OF EMPLOYEES	MAJOR PRODUCT/SERVICE	ORGANIZATION TYPE
206-555-2927	40	restaurant	s

CLIENT ACCOUNT FORM 051

Quantum Corporation

[X] ADD [ ] MODIFY [ ] DELETE

ACCOUNT NUMBER	NAME	REPRESENTATIVE (Last Name)
00505	West Coast Hardware Supplies	Sharpe

INDEXED NAME

ADDRESS	CITY	STATE	ZIP
4485 Beacon Avenue West	Seattle	WA	98108

PHONE	NO. OF EMPLOYEES	MAJOR PRODUCT/SERVICE	ORGANIZATION TYPE
206-555-4992	325	hardware	w

CLIENT ACCOUNT FORM 052

Quantum Corporation

[X] ADD [ ] MODIFY [ ] DELETE

ACCOUNT NUMBER	NAME	REPRESENTATIVE (Last Name)
00509	West Coast Department Stores, Inc.	Lyle

INDEXED NAME

ADDRESS	CITY	STATE	ZIP
1100 6th Avenue	Santa Rosa	CA	95422

PHONE	NO. OF EMPLOYEES	MAJOR PRODUCT/SERVICE	ORGANIZATION TYPE
707-555-8245	540	department stores	r

CLIENT ACCOUNT FORM 053

Quantum Corporation

[X] ADD [ ] MODIFY [ ] DELETE

ACCOUNT NUMBER	NAME	REPRESENTATIVE (Last Name)
00520	Tiny Tots Day Care Centers	Sharpe

INDEXED NAME

ADDRESS	CITY	STATE	ZIP
15601 Pacific Highway West	Seattle	WA	98188

PHONE	NO. OF EMPLOYEES	MAJOR PRODUCT/SERVICE	ORGANIZATION TYPE
206-555-0220	15	day care	s

CLIENT ACCOUNT FORM 054

Quantum Corporation

[X] ADD [ ] MODIFY [ ] DELETE

ACCOUNT NUMBER	NAME	REPRESENTATIVE (Last Name)
00560	Verona Lumber Co.	Nelson

INDEXED NAME

ADDRESS	CITY	STATE	ZIP
219 1/2 Sprague Avenue	Spokane	WA	99204

PHONE	NO. OF EMPLOYEES	MAJOR PRODUCT/SERVICE	ORGANIZATION TYPE
509-555-2672	145	lumber	m

CLIENT ACCOUNT FORM 055

Quantum Corporation

[X] ADD [ ] MODIFY [ ] DELETE

ACCOUNT NUMBER	NAME	REPRESENTATIVE (Last Name)
00571	Tykes Centers of America	Price

INDEXED NAME

ADDRESS	CITY	STATE	ZIP
10295 Le Conte Avenue	Los Angeles	CA	90024

PHONE	NO. OF EMPLOYEES	MAJOR PRODUCT/SERVICE	ORGANIZATION TYPE
213-555-8033	1055	day care	s

CLIENT ACCOUNT FORM 056

Quantum Corporation

[X] ADD [ ] MODIFY [ ] DELETE

ACCOUNT NUMBER	NAME	REPRESENTATIVE (Last Name)
00600	Stockton Dairies	Treat

INDEXED NAME

ADDRESS	CITY	STATE	ZIP
380 Post Road	San Francisco	CA	94108

PHONE	NO. OF EMPLOYEES	MAJOR PRODUCT/SERVICE	ORGANIZATION TYPE
415-555-0932	320	dairy products	m

CLIENT ACCOUNT FORM

Quantum Corporation

057

[X] ADD   [ ] MODIFY   [ ] DELETE

ACCOUNT NUMBER	NAME	REPRESENTATIVE (Last Name)
00550	Roberts Transfer	Sharpe

INDEXED NAME

ADDRESS	CITY	STATE	ZIP
1400 4th Avenue	Seattle	WA	98101

PHONE	NO. OF EMPLOYEES	MAJOR PRODUCT/SERVICE	ORGANIZATION TYPE
206-555-9023	410	trucking	s

CLIENT ACCOUNT FORM

Quantum Corporation

058

[X] ADD   [ ] MODIFY   [ ] DELETE

ACCOUNT NUMBER	NAME	REPRESENTATIVE (Last Name)
00610	Smithson Wholesalers	Eberhard

INDEXED NAME

ADDRESS	CITY	STATE	ZIP
240 Kenyon	San Diego	CA	92110

PHONE	NO. OF EMPLOYEES	MAJOR PRODUCT/SERVICE	ORGANIZATION TYPE
619-555-2120	450	gifts	w

CLIENT ACCOUNT FORM

Quantum Corporation

059

[X] ADD   [ ] MODIFY   [ ] DELETE

ACCOUNT NUMBER	NAME	REPRESENTATIVE (Last Name)
00630	Vista Vogue Boutique	Lyle

INDEXED NAME

ADDRESS	CITY	STATE	ZIP
4500 Hollywood Boulevard	Los Angeles	CA	90027

PHONE	NO. OF EMPLOYEES	MAJOR PRODUCT/SERVICE	ORGANIZATION TYPE
213-555-3930	5	clothing	r

CLIENT ACCOUNT FORM

Quantum Corporation

060

[X] ADD   [ ] MODIFY   [ ] DELETE

ACCOUNT NUMBER	NAME	REPRESENTATIVE (Last Name)
10015	Reliable Rentals	Price

INDEXED NAME

ADDRESS	CITY	STATE	ZIP
550 North Weber Drive	Fresno	CA	93728

PHONE	NO. OF EMPLOYEES	MAJOR PRODUCT/SERVICE	ORGANIZATION TYPE
209-555-9652	25	auto rentals	s

CLIENT ACCOUNT FORM

Quantum Corporation

061

☐ ADD ☒ MODIFY ☐ DELETE

ACCOUNT NUMBER	NAME	REPRESENTATIVE (Last Name)
	R and R Travel Service, Inc.	

INDEXED NAME

ADDRESS	CITY	STATE	ZIP
961 North View Avenue			

PHONE	NO. OF EMPLOYEES	MAJOR PRODUCT/SERVICE	ORGANIZATION TYPE
619-555-0193			

CLIENT ACCOUNT FORM

Quantum Corporation

062

☐ ADD ☒ MODIFY ☐ DELETE

ACCOUNT NUMBER	NAME	REPRESENTATIVE (Last Name)
	Wake Co Manufacturing	

INDEXED NAME

ADDRESS	CITY	STATE	ZIP

PHONE	NO. OF EMPLOYEES	MAJOR PRODUCT/SERVICE	ORGANIZATION TYPE
	599		

CLIENT ACCOUNT FORM

Quantum Corporation

063

☐ ADD ☒ MODIFY ☐ DELETE

ACCOUNT NUMBER	NAME	REPRESENTATIVE (Last Name)
00262		

INDEXED NAME

ADDRESS	CITY	STATE	ZIP

PHONE	NO. OF EMPLOYEES	MAJOR PRODUCT/SERVICE	ORGANIZATION TYPE
		ground transportation	

CLIENT ACCOUNT FORM

Quantum Corporation

064

☐ ADD ☒ MODIFY ☐ DELETE

ACCOUNT NUMBER	NAME	REPRESENTATIVE (Last Name)
00571	Tykes Centers of America	

INDEXED NAME

ADDRESS	CITY	STATE	ZIP

PHONE	NO. OF EMPLOYEES	MAJOR PRODUCT/SERVICE	ORGANIZATION TYPE
	1029		

Quantum Corporation

CLIENT ACCOUNT FORM 065

☐ ADD ☐ MODIFY ☒ DELETE

ACCOUNT NUMBER	NAME	REPRESENTATIVE (Last Name)
00472		

INDEXED NAME

| | | | |

ADDRESS	CITY	STATE	ZIP

PHONE	NO. OF EMPLOYEES	MAJOR PRODUCT/SERVICE	ORGANIZATION TYPE

Quantum Corporation

CLIENT ACCOUNT FORM 066

☐ ADD ☐ MODIFY ☒ DELETE

ACCOUNT NUMBER	NAME	REPRESENTATIVE (Last Name)
00032		

INDEXED NAME

ADDRESS	CITY	STATE	ZIP

PHONE	NO. OF EMPLOYEES	MAJOR PRODUCT/SERVICE	ORGANIZATION TYPE

Quantum Corporation

CLIENT ACCOUNT FORM 067

☐ ADD ☐ MODIFY ☒ DELETE

ACCOUNT NUMBER	NAME	REPRESENTATIVE (Last Name)
00600		

INDEXED NAME

ADDRESS	CITY	STATE	ZIP

PHONE	NO. OF EMPLOYEES	MAJOR PRODUCT/SERVICE	ORGANIZATION TYPE

Quantum Corporation

CLIENT ACCOUNT FORM 068

☐ ADD ☐ MODIFY ☒ DELETE

ACCOUNT NUMBER	NAME	REPRESENTATIVE (Last Name)
00560		

INDEXED NAME

ADDRESS	CITY	STATE	ZIP

PHONE	NO. OF EMPLOYEES	MAJOR PRODUCT/SERVICE	ORGANIZATION TYPE

CLIENT ACCOUNT FORM 069

Quantum Corporation

☐ ADD   ☒ MODIFY   ☐ DELETE

ACCOUNT NUMBER	NAME Saxton Distributors	REPRESENTATIVE (Last Name)

INDEXED NAME																							

ADDRESS	CITY	STATE	ZIP

PHONE 415-555-9187	NO. OF EMPLOYEES	MAJOR PRODUCT/SERVICE	ORGANIZATION TYPE

CLIENT ACCOUNT FORM 070

Quantum Corporation

☐ ADD   ☒ MODIFY   ☐ DELETE

ACCOUNT NUMBER	NAME The Safe Way	REPRESENTATIVE (Last Name)

INDEXED NAME																							

ADDRESS	CITY	STATE	ZIP

PHONE	NO. OF EMPLOYEES	MAJOR PRODUCT/SERVICE guard service	ORGANIZATION TYPE

CLIENT ACCOUNT FORM 071

Quantum Corporation

☐ ADD   ☒ MODIFY   ☐ DELETE

ACCOUNT NUMBER 00255	NAME	REPRESENTATIVE (Last Name)

INDEXED NAME																							

ADDRESS	CITY	STATE	ZIP

PHONE	NO. OF EMPLOYEES 38	MAJOR PRODUCT/SERVICE	ORGANIZATION TYPE

CLIENT ACCOUNT FORM 072

Quantum Corporation

☐ ADD   ☒ MODIFY   ☐ DELETE

ACCOUNT NUMBER	NAME R. T. Stanley Manufacturers	REPRESENTATIVE (Last Name)

INDEXED NAME																							

ADDRESS	CITY	STATE	ZIP

PHONE	NO. OF EMPLOYEES 2100	MAJOR PRODUCT/SERVICE	ORGANIZATION TYPE

CLIENT ACCOUNT FORM

Quantum Corporation   073

[X] ADD   [ ] MODIFY   [ ] DELETE

ACCOUNT NUMBER	NAME	REPRESENTATIVE (Last Name)
10020	West Coast National Bank	Price

INDEXED NAME

ADDRESS	CITY	STATE	ZIP
256 Market Street	San Diego	CA	92110

PHONE	NO. OF EMPLOYEES	MAJOR PRODUCT/SERVICE	ORGANIZATION TYPE
619-555-5892	248	bank	s

CLIENT ACCOUNT FORM

Quantum Corporation   074

[X] ADD   [ ] MODIFY   [ ] DELETE

ACCOUNT NUMBER	NAME	REPRESENTATIVE (Last Name)
10025	Sandra's Seafood Restaurant	Sharpe

INDEXED NAME

ADDRESS	CITY	STATE	ZIP
451 Bay Shore Drive	Seattle	WA	98101

PHONE	NO. OF EMPLOYEES	MAJOR PRODUCT/SERVICE	ORGANIZATION TYPE
206-555-2316	44	restaurant	s

CLIENT ACCOUNT FORM

Quantum Corporation   075

[X] ADD   [ ] MODIFY   [ ] DELETE

ACCOUNT NUMBER	NAME	REPRESENTATIVE (Last Name)
10030	The Research Foundation	Nelson

INDEXED NAME

ADDRESS	CITY	STATE	ZIP
200 East Water Street	Portland	OR	97205

PHONE	NO. OF EMPLOYEES	MAJOR PRODUCT/SERVICE	ORGANIZATION TYPE
503-555-8621	256	medical research	n

CLIENT ACCOUNT FORM

Quantum Corporation   076

[X] ADD   [ ] MODIFY   [ ] DELETE

ACCOUNT NUMBER	NAME	REPRESENTATIVE (Last Name)
10035	Tykes Centers of America	Sharpe

INDEXED NAME

ADDRESS	CITY	STATE	ZIP
3003 Battleship Boulevard	Seattle	WA	98101

PHONE	NO. OF EMPLOYEES	MAJOR PRODUCT/SERVICE	ORGANIZATION TYPE
206-555-3033	12	day care	s

Quantum Corporation — CLIENT ACCOUNT FORM 077

[X] ADD [ ] MODIFY [ ] DELETE

ACCOUNT NUMBER	NAME	REPRESENTATIVE (Last Name)
00012	Vannessa's Cosmetics	Treat

INDEXED NAME

ADDRESS	CITY	STATE	ZIP
345 West Lincoln	Anaheim	CA	92805

PHONE	NO. OF EMPLOYEES	MAJOR PRODUCT/SERVICE	ORGANIZATION TYPE
213-555-3232	600	cosmetics	m

Quantum Corporation — CLIENT ACCOUNT FORM 078

[X] ADD [ ] MODIFY [ ] DELETE

ACCOUNT NUMBER	NAME	REPRESENTATIVE (Last Name)
00015	The Red Cross	Holmes

INDEXED NAME

ADDRESS	CITY	STATE	ZIP
245 South Westchester Drive	Anaheim	CA	92804

PHONE	NO. OF EMPLOYEES	MAJOR PRODUCT/SERVICE	ORGANIZATION TYPE
213-555-8911	45	disaster relief	n

Quantum Corporation — CLIENT ACCOUNT FORM 079

[X] ADD [ ] MODIFY [ ] DELETE

ACCOUNT NUMBER	NAME	REPRESENTATIVE (Last Name)
00022	Serve n' Save	Lyle

INDEXED NAME

ADDRESS	CITY	STATE	ZIP
401 34th Street	Bakersfield	CA	93301

PHONE	NO. OF EMPLOYEES	MAJOR PRODUCT/SERVICE	ORGANIZATION TYPE
805-555-6868	500	gasoline	r

Quantum Corporation — CLIENT ACCOUNT FORM 080

[X] ADD [ ] MODIFY [ ] DELETE

ACCOUNT NUMBER	NAME	REPRESENTATIVE (Last Name)
00025	T J Investments, Inc.	Price

INDEXED NAME

ADDRESS	CITY	STATE	ZIP
205 Chester	Bakersfield	CA	93301

PHONE	NO. OF EMPLOYEES	MAJOR PRODUCT/SERVICE	ORGANIZATION TYPE
805-555-2405	150	investments	s

Quantum Corporation — CLIENT ACCOUNT FORM — 081

☒ ADD ☐ MODIFY ☐ DELETE

ACCOUNT NUMBER	NAME	REPRESENTATIVE (Last Name)
00028	U.S. Postal Service	Treat

INDEXED NAME

ADDRESS	CITY	STATE	ZIP
800 Truxton	Bakersfield	CA	93301

PHONE	NO. OF EMPLOYEES	MAJOR PRODUCT/SERVICE	ORGANIZATION TYPE
805-555-2509	50	postal service	g

Quantum Corporation — CLIENT ACCOUNT FORM — 082

☒ ADD ☐ MODIFY ☐ DELETE

ACCOUNT NUMBER	NAME	REPRESENTATIVE (Last Name)
00035	WTQR TV	Price

INDEXED NAME

ADDRESS	CITY	STATE	ZIP
8420 Sunset Boulevard	Los Angeles	CA	90069

PHONE	NO. OF EMPLOYEES	MAJOR PRODUCT/SERVICE	ORGANIZATION TYPE
213-555-2734	50	television	s

Quantum Corporation — CLIENT ACCOUNT FORM — 083

☒ ADD ☐ MODIFY ☐ DELETE

ACCOUNT NUMBER	NAME	REPRESENTATIVE (Last Name)
00040	Wondra Health Spas, Inc.	Price

INDEXED NAME

ADDRESS	CITY	STATE	ZIP
770 South Broadway	Los Angeles	CA	90013

PHONE	NO. OF EMPLOYEES	MAJOR PRODUCT/SERVICE	ORGANIZATION TYPE
213-555-2393	65	health spa	s

Quantum Corporation — CLIENT ACCOUNT FORM — 084

☒ ADD ☐ MODIFY ☐ DELETE

ACCOUNT NUMBER	NAME	REPRESENTATIVE (Last Name)
00052	Tax Consultants Unlimited	Price

INDEXED NAME

ADDRESS	CITY	STATE	ZIP
6402 West Sunset Boulevard	Los Angeles	CA	90028

PHONE	NO. OF EMPLOYEES	MAJOR PRODUCT/SERVICE	ORGANIZATION TYPE
213-555-8933	150	tax preparation	s

CLIENT ACCOUNT FORM 085

Quantum Corporation

[X] ADD [ ] MODIFY [ ] DELETE

ACCOUNT NUMBER	NAME	REPRESENTATIVE (Last Name)
00120	Rest EZ Waterbeds	Lyle

INDEXED NAME

ADDRESS	CITY	STATE	ZIP
4700 East Kings Canyon Road	Fresno	CA	93702

PHONE	NO. OF EMPLOYEES	MAJOR PRODUCT/SERVICE	ORGANIZATION TYPE
209-555-6592	550	waterbeds/furniture	r

CLIENT ACCOUNT FORM 086

Quantum Corporation

[X] ADD [ ] MODIFY [ ] DELETE

ACCOUNT NUMBER	NAME	REPRESENTATIVE (Last Name)
00132	Oregon Division of Motor Vehicles	Nelson

INDEXED NAME

ADDRESS	CITY	STATE	ZIP
2570 24th Street	Portland	OR	97205

PHONE	NO. OF EMPLOYEES	MAJOR PRODUCT/SERVICE	ORGANIZATION TYPE
503-555-7878	350	vehicle registration	g

CLIENT ACCOUNT FORM 087

Quantum Corporation

[X] ADD [ ] MODIFY [ ] DELETE

ACCOUNT NUMBER	NAME	REPRESENTATIVE (Last Name)
00144	The Very One Gifts	Lyle

INDEXED NAME

ADDRESS	CITY	STATE	ZIP
1920 El Cajon Boulevard	San Diego	CA	92104

PHONE	NO. OF EMPLOYEES	MAJOR PRODUCT/SERVICE	ORGANIZATION TYPE
619-555-9291	45	gifts	r

CLIENT ACCOUNT FORM 088

Quantum Corporation

[X] ADD [ ] MODIFY [ ] DELETE

ACCOUNT NUMBER	NAME	REPRESENTATIVE (Last Name)
00155	Rogers-Perkins Funeral Homes	Price

INDEXED NAME

ADDRESS	CITY	STATE	ZIP
110 Pine Street	San Francisco	CA	94111

PHONE	NO. OF EMPLOYEES	MAJOR PRODUCT/SERVICE	ORGANIZATION TYPE
414-555-6724	75	funeral home	s

CLIENT ACCOUNT FORM 089

Quantum Corporation

[X] ADD [ ] MODIFY [ ] DELETE

ACCOUNT NUMBER	NAME	REPRESENTATIVE (Last Name)
00163	Salvation Tabernacle	Holmes

INDEXED NAME

ADDRESS	CITY	STATE	ZIP
650 Market Street	San Francisco	CA	94102

PHONE	NO. OF EMPLOYEES	MAJOR PRODUCT/SERVICE	ORGANIZATION TYPE
415-555-3494	65	food & shelter	n

CLIENT ACCOUNT FORM 090

Quantum Corporation

[X] ADD [ ] MODIFY [ ] DELETE

ACCOUNT NUMBER	NAME	REPRESENTATIVE (Last Name)
00164	Woman's Clubs of America	Holmes

INDEXED NAME

ADDRESS	CITY	STATE	ZIP
35 Mission	San Francisco	CA	94119

PHONE	NO. OF EMPLOYEES	MAJOR PRODUCT/SERVICE	ORGANIZATION TYPE
415-555-8921	45	service club	n

CLIENT ACCOUNT FORM 091

Quantum Corporation

[X] ADD [ ] MODIFY [ ] DELETE

ACCOUNT NUMBER	NAME	REPRESENTATIVE (Last Name)
00172	Safe-Guards Unlimited	Price

INDEXED NAME

ADDRESS	CITY	STATE	ZIP
1000 Market Street	San Francisco	CA	94105

PHONE	NO. OF EMPLOYEES	MAJOR PRODUCT/SERVICE	ORGANIZATION TYPE
415-555-2552	70	guard service	s

CLIENT ACCOUNT FORM 092

Quantum Corporation

[X] ADD [ ] MODIFY [ ] DELETE

ACCOUNT NUMBER	NAME	REPRESENTATIVE (Last Name)
00187	Trouble Help Line	Holmes

INDEXED NAME

ADDRESS	CITY	STATE	ZIP
455 Battery	San Francisco	CA	94111

PHONE	NO. OF EMPLOYEES	MAJOR PRODUCT/SERVICE	ORGANIZATION TYPE
415-555-2390	30	emerg. tele. serv.	n

Quantum Corporation — CLIENT ACCOUNT FORM 093

☒ ADD ☐ MODIFY ☐ DELETE

ACCOUNT NUMBER	NAME	REPRESENTATIVE (Last Name)
00201	Roper Industries	Treat

INDEXED NAME

ADDRESS	CITY	STATE	ZIP
500 Stockton Street	San Francisco	CA	94106

PHONE	NO. OF EMPLOYEES	MAJOR PRODUCT/SERVICE	ORGANIZATION TYPE
415-555-2861	420	elec. components	m

Quantum Corporation — CLIENT ACCOUNT FORM 094

☒ ADD ☐ MODIFY ☐ DELETE

ACCOUNT NUMBER	NAME	REPRESENTATIVE (Last Name)
00210	U.S. Federal Bankruptcy Court	Treat

INDEXED NAME

ADDRESS	CITY	STATE	ZIP
50 Fulton Avenue	San Francisco	CA	94102

PHONE	NO. OF EMPLOYEES	MAJOR PRODUCT/SERVICE	ORGANIZATION TYPE
415-555-5103	315	court of law	g

Quantum Corporation — CLIENT ACCOUNT FORM 095

☒ ADD ☐ MODIFY ☐ DELETE

ACCOUNT NUMBER	NAME	REPRESENTATIVE (Last Name)
00215	Roman Spas, Inc.	Price

INDEXED NAME

ADDRESS	CITY	STATE	ZIP
115 Pine Street	San Francisco	CA	94111

PHONE	NO. OF EMPLOYEES	MAJOR PRODUCT/SERVICE	ORGANIZATION TYPE
415-555-2328	700	health spa	s

Quantum Corporation — CLIENT ACCOUNT FORM 096

☒ ADD ☐ MODIFY ☐ DELETE

ACCOUNT NUMBER	NAME	REPRESENTATIVE (Last Name)
00297	U.S. Court House	Treat

INDEXED NAME

ADDRESS	CITY	STATE	ZIP
920 West Riverside Drive	Bakersfield	CA	93301

PHONE	NO. OF EMPLOYEES	MAJOR PRODUCT/SERVICE	ORGANIZATION TYPE
805-555-2420	230	court of law	g

CLIENT ACCOUNT FORM

Quantum Corporation

097

[X] ADD [ ] MODIFY [ ] DELETE

ACCOUNT NUMBER	NAME	REPRESENTATIVE (Last Name)
00451	Seattle Vocational Training Center	Sharpe

INDEXED NAME

ADDRESS	CITY	STATE	ZIP
1004 3d Avenue	Seattle	WA	98101

PHONE	NO. OF EMPLOYEES	MAJOR PRODUCT/SERVICE	ORGANIZATION TYPE
206-555-5401	125	school	s

CLIENT ACCOUNT FORM

Quantum Corporation

098

[X] ADD [ ] MODIFY [ ] DELETE

ACCOUNT NUMBER	NAME	REPRESENTATIVE (Last Name)
00454	Seashore National Bank	Sharpe

INDEXED NAME

ADDRESS	CITY	STATE	ZIP
400 Seneca Way	Seattle	WA	98111

PHONE	NO. OF EMPLOYEES	MAJOR PRODUCT/SERVICE	ORGANIZATION TYPE
206-555-6462	890	bank	s

CLIENT ACCOUNT FORM

Quantum Corporation

099

[X] ADD [ ] MODIFY [ ] DELETE

ACCOUNT NUMBER	NAME	REPRESENTATIVE (Last Name)
00462	U.S. Department of the Interior	Sharpe

INDEXED NAME

ADDRESS	CITY	STATE	ZIP
Richmond Beach Bridge	Seattle	WA	98160

PHONE	NO. OF EMPLOYEES	MAJOR PRODUCT/SERVICE	ORGANIZATION TYPE
206-555-2307	180	public rec. area	g

CLIENT ACCOUNT FORM

Quantum Corporation

100

[X] ADD [ ] MODIFY [ ] DELETE

ACCOUNT NUMBER	NAME	REPRESENTATIVE (Last Name)
00489	Video Vue	Price

INDEXED NAME

ADDRESS	CITY	STATE	ZIP
315 1st Avenue	Fresno	CA	93728

PHONE	NO. OF EMPLOYEES	MAJOR PRODUCT/SERVICE	ORGANIZATION TYPE
209-555-9821	90	video rentals	s

Quantum Corporation — CLIENT ACCOUNT FORM 101

[X] ADD   [ ] MODIFY   [ ] DELETE

ACCOUNT NUMBER	NAME	REPRESENTATIVE (Last Name)
00494	Varner Trucking Co.	Sharpe

INDEXED NAME

ADDRESS	CITY	STATE	ZIP
81 Columbia Pike	Seattle	WA	98104

PHONE	NO. OF EMPLOYEES	MAJOR PRODUCT/SERVICE	ORGANIZATION TYPE
206-555-6566	240	trucking	s

Quantum Corporation — CLIENT ACCOUNT FORM 102

[X] ADD   [ ] MODIFY   [ ] DELETE

ACCOUNT NUMBER	NAME	REPRESENTATIVE (Last Name)
00513	Underwood Garments, Inc.	Sharpe

INDEXED NAME

ADDRESS	CITY	STATE	ZIP
701 North Union	Seattle	WA	98101

PHONE	NO. OF EMPLOYEES	MAJOR PRODUCT/SERVICE	ORGANIZATION TYPE
206-555-8420	750	clothing	m

Quantum Corporation — CLIENT ACCOUNT FORM 103

[X] ADD   [ ] MODIFY   [ ] DELETE

ACCOUNT NUMBER	NAME	REPRESENTATIVE (Last Name)
00570	Thomas Reed Stores, Inc.	Lyle

INDEXED NAME

ADDRESS	CITY	STATE	ZIP
8000 Vermont Avenue	Los Angeles	CA	90044

PHONE	NO. OF EMPLOYEES	MAJOR PRODUCT/SERVICE	ORGANIZATION TYPE
213-555-6620	450	department stores	r

Quantum Corporation — CLIENT ACCOUNT FORM 104

[X] ADD   [ ] MODIFY   [ ] DELETE

ACCOUNT NUMBER	NAME	REPRESENTATIVE (Last Name)
00590	The Williams' Group	Price

INDEXED NAME

ADDRESS	CITY	STATE	ZIP
500 Market	San Francisco	CA	94103

PHONE	NO. OF EMPLOYEES	MAJOR PRODUCT/SERVICE	ORGANIZATION TYPE
415-555-2405	95	financial advice	s

UNIT IV

QUANTUM CORPORATION INVENTORY FILE

Quantum Corporation has an inventory of office equipment, located in various departments, that must be carefully maintained. The managers have experienced difficulty with the scheduling of office equipment maintenance and replacement. Maintenance and repair records have been kept haphazardly and are inaccurate.

The computerized employee and client files in Units II and III operated very well. The managers have now decided to convert to a computerized inventory database file for more efficient scheduling of service and handling of repairs.

In creating this file, much thought went into choosing the key field. You will recall from the Overview that every record must contain a key field so information can be retrieved from the file. The key field must be unique for each record. After deciding which fields were to be included in this file, the managers' first thought was to use the serial number of each item of equipment. Then they realized that whereas serial numbers are unique for each manufacturer's separate equipment items, different manufacturers might use the same numbers. So they decided to assign a unique item code to each piece of office equipment owned by Quantum. The first two characters of this code are letters which stand for the kind of equipment. For example, the letters *TY* mean that the item is a typewriter. The last two characters are digits which are unique for each kind of equipment. For example, all electronic typewriters owned by the company are assigned a two-digit number of their own such as 01 or 02. This makes the key field both descriptive and unique **(TY01, TY02).**

Creating the File

Name _____ Date _____

Section _____ Evaluation _____

In this exercise you will design and create your file. Remember the suggestions made in the first three units for doing this.

One of the first things to do is name your database file. You should check your software manual for naming rules. Many software packages limit you to eight-character names with the first character being a letter. Generally, you are not allowed to include spaces in a filename. An important rule is to always make your database name descriptive so that your file can be easily identified.

Next you will work with the fields. Each field will also be named. Again, you may be limited to a few characters, and you should make the field name describe the field. Be consistent. For example, you might choose to prefix each field name in the inventory file with the letters *INV* (**INVCODE, INVNAME**).

With many software packages it is possible to lay out your screen to match your input (source) document. In any case, you should arrange the fields in the same sequence as the source document so that the person entering the data can do it quickly and easily.

It is important to be aware of the field type when designing your database. Look at the data and think about the ways in which you will be required to use it. If you think a field might be used for mathematical calculations, it must be a numeric field. If the field will be used for logical decisions, it should be a logical field.

When you lay out your input screen, you must know the length of each field. Examine the data and determine the item in each field with the greatest number of characters. Decide whether this is likely to be the maximum possible length. Make the field the maximum length. Also decide whether you can save space and keystrokes with some data fields by *coding* the entry. (For example, in a student database, a full-time student could be coded as *F* and a part-time student as *P*.)

When keying dates, remember to use a format that will allow sorting. Also, it is wise to separate two date fields from one another by another field. This makes the record easier to read on the screen.

EXERCISE 77

Entering the Data

Name _____ Date _____

Section _____ Evaluation _____

Quantum Corporation has manually maintained an equipment inventory for all departments in a centrally located file. The decision to convert this manual filing system to a computerized system will improve control of computer maintenance and service costs.

The office manager has prepared an Equipment Inventory List of all equipment owned by Quantum. In preparation for computer input, remove this list, which is on page 000, and refer to it as you read the following information about each column.

ITEM CODE. The office manager has assigned each piece of equipment a unique code which will serve as the key field in this file. Refer to the Item Code column of the Equipment Inventory List. Note that each Item Code has two letters followed by two digits. The two letters stand for the type of equipment, and the two digits stand for the individual machine within that type of equipment. For example, the third (03) electronic typewriter (TY) is the piece of equipment with an item code of **TY03**.

ITEM NAME. Item Name is the type of equipment in inventory.

DEPT. Quantum has three departments: administration, research, and sales.

DATE P/L. This is the date on which the equipment was either purchased or leased.

P/L. This column has a *P* (uppercase) if the equipment was purchased or *L* (uppercase) if it was leased.

EXPIR. DATE. This is the day and month on which the annual warranty or service contract on the equipment expires or ends.

SERIAL NO. This is the identification code marked on each piece of equipment by the manufacturer.

COST. This is the amount paid for the purchased equipment or the fair-market value of the leased equipment.

SERVICE VENDOR. This is the business selected to make any repair or service required to keep the equipment in good working condition.

LAST SERVICE DATE. This is the date on which the equipment was last serviced or repaired.

MANUFACTURER. The manufacturer is the company that produced the equipment.

Key the data for Quantum's equipment inventory into the database file you created using the Equipment Inventory List. Proofread each record after it is keyed.

QUANTUM CORPORATION
INVENTORY FILE

Listing the Records in the Database

Name _____   Date _____

Section _____   Evaluation _____

Sort the file by Item Code; then print a copy of the file listing all data in every record. Use as few sheets of paper as possible. Proofread the file again, checking the printout against the original Equipment Inventory List.

Writing a Program/Macro

Name _____   Date _____

Section _____   Evaluation _____

In order to assist with ease of data entry, some repetitive tasks can be programmed. This allows you to complete an operation with a few keystrokes. One of the tasks you will perform often when using any database is a lookup or search. In most searches you specify a condition by naming your input criterion or data field, your logical or relational operator (such as =, >, <, >=, <=, <>), and your output criterion or search object.

If your database software allows it, write a program or macro that will list all the records that have a value equal to your search criterion. In your program, prompt the user for the name of the input criterion or data field. Then prompt the user for the output criterion or search object. Then locate the record or records that match your search criterion and display them on the monitor.

Note: This is a good exercise for Lotus users.

dBASE III+ users should write a program that will list all the records with an Item Code value equal to your search criterion. Prompt the user for the Item Code you wish displayed. Then list the Item Code, Item Name, and Serial Number of the record that matches your search criterion.

QUANTUM CORPORATION
INVENTORY FILE

Searching for Service Vendors

Name _____   Date _____

Section _____   Evaluation _____

The administrative assistant of the administration department has asked for the following information to verify billing records.

a. How many items of equipment are serviced by City Computer Repair?

_____

b. How many items of equipment are serviced by Supra Machine Repair?

_____

c. How many items of equipment are serviced by Best Key Service?

_____

d. How many items of equipment are serviced by Venus Repair?

_____

Adding Records

Name _____ Date _____

Section _____ Evaluation _____

The research director recently requested the purchase of two additional calculators for use in research; two new electronic calculators have been received. These two calculators have never been serviced or repaired, so leave the Last Service Date field blank.

Add the records to the file.

ITEM CODE	ITEM NAME	DEPT.	DATE P/L	P/L	EXPIR. DATE	SERIAL NO.
EC05	Electronic Calculator	Research	92/06/15	P	12/31	RR43448
EC06	Electronic Calculator	Research	92/06/15	P	12/31	RS654344

COST	SERVICE VENDOR	MANUFACTURER
539.00	Supra Machine Repair	Electrocom
539.00	Supra Machine Repair	Electrocom

Printing Computer Equipment in Report Form

Name _____ Date _____

Section _____ Evaluation _____

The office manager requests a list of computer equipment in each department for an internal audit.

Title the report *Computer Equipment Inventory.* Arrange by department and select the computer equipment by looking for *CP* as the first and second characters in the Item Code field. In the report, include data for the item code and name, department, date purchased/leased, whether the item was purchased or leased, the expiration date, and cost. Decide on appropriate columnar headings for your report. Provide a subtotal of the cost of equipment in each department and a count of the number of items in each department.

Finding Equipment Needing Service

Name _____ Date _____

Section _____ Evaluation _____

Find and list the item numbers of all the equipment which will need to be serviced this month.

Hint: Quantum has all equipment serviced every six months, so you will need to look at the last service date. Choose those that were serviced six months ago.

Item Nos: _____

Searching for Expiration Dates

Name _____   Date _____

Section _____   Evaluation _____

The expiration date represents the month and day on which the annual warranty or service contract will expire. Before a warranty or service contract expires, Quantum routinely has its equipment checked to make sure that it is in good working order. If anything is wrong, it will have to be repaired before the contract expiration date.

The administrative assistant to the office manager requests the following information:

a. On which items will the warranty or service contract expire in June? Report item code, department, and expiration date for each.

ITEM CODE	DEPARTMENT	EXPIRATION DATE

b. On which items will the warranty or service contract expire in July? Report item code, department, and expiration date for each.

ITEM CODE	DEPARTMENT	EXPIRATION DATE

QUANTUM CORPORATION
INVENTORY FILE

EXERCISE 85

Helping the Office Manager

Name _____ Date _____

Section _____ Evaluation _____

The office manager requests information needed to complete a five-year plan for new equipment purchases. Quantum replaces equipment according to its age and frequency of use.

a. How many pieces of equipment were purchased or leased before 91/01/01?

_____

b. How many pieces of equipment were purchased or leased before 90/01/01?

_____

c. How many pieces of computer equipment (item code beginning with *CP*) were purchased or leased before 90/01/01?

_____

EXERCISE 86

Updating Records

Name _____ Date _____

Section _____ Evaluation _____

A typewriter repairer from Best Key Service has left a service report for a visit made on 94/03/05.

Update the Last Service Date field for all equipment serviced by Best Key Service.

124

Altering the Database

Name _____   Date _____

Section _____   Evaluation _____

The decision has been made to add two new fields to the file: one to show the monthly rental price for leased equipment and another to give the monthly service contract price, where applicable, for all equipment. Add these two fields and update the records as follows:

ITEM	LEASE	SERVICE
CP01	49.50	
CP02	269.00	
CP03		6.00
CP04		6.00
CP05	57.00	4.00
CP06	57.00	4.00
CP07	42.50	4.00
CP08	42.50	4.00
CP09	42.50	4.00
CP10	60.00	8.00
CP11	59.00	4.00
PC01		15.00
PC02		8.00
TY01		2.00
TY02		2.00
TY03		2.00
TY04		2.00
TY05		2.00
TY06		2.00

EXERCISE 88

Deleting Records

Name _____   Date _____

Section _____   Evaluation _____

The office manager has sent a memo to let you know that the items AD01 and PC01 are being taken out of service because they are no longer needed. This equipment is old, outdated, inadequate, and constantly in need of repair. They will both be replaced with more modern equipment at a later date.

Delete these two items from the file.

EXERCISE 89

Finding Equipment Value

Name _____   Date _____

Section _____   Evaluation _____

The accountant has requested the following information to complete the internal audit started earlier by the office manager. Calculate the equipment value by adding the cost of each item.

a. Total value of equipment in the administration department: _____

b. Total value of equipment in the research department: _____

c. Total value of equipment in the sales department: _____

d. Total value of all equipment: _____

Answering Inquiries

Name _____   Date _____

Section _____   Evaluation _____

The information resources manager phoned and asked the following questions.

a. How many pieces of computer equipment are being leased? _____

b. How many pieces of computer equipment were purchased? _____

c. Who is the service vendor for the central processing unit of the computer, item CP02? _____

d. Who is the service vendor for the computer modem, item CP01? _____

_____

e. Who is the service vendor for the laser printer? _____

127

Adding Records

Name _____   Date _____

Section _____   Evaluation _____

The information resources manager has leased four computer terminals to be used for word processing in the three departments.

Add the records for these computer terminals to the file. The terminals have not been used enough to require service, so leave the Last Service Date field blank.

ITEM CODE	ITEM NAME	DEPT.	DATE P/L	P/L	EXPIR. DATE	SERIAL NO.
CP12	Computer Terminal	Research	92/08/01	L	95/08/01	T775842
CP13	Computer Terminal	Sales	92/08/01	L	95/08/01	T875944
CP14	Computer Terminal	Admin.	92/08/01	L	95/08/01	T887654
CP15	Computer Terminal	Research	92/08/01	L	95/08/01	T997865

COST	SERVICE VENDOR	MANUFACTURER	MONTHLY LEASE	MONTHLY SERVICE
2775.00	City Computer Repair	Digiquip	37.50	4.00
2775.00	City Computer Repair	Digiquip	37.50	4.00
2775.00	City Computer Repair	Digiquip	37.50	4.00
2775.00	City Computer Repair	Digiquip	37.50	4.00

QUANTUM CORPORATION
INVENTORY FILE

Helping the Accountant

Name _____   Date _____

Section _____   Evaluation _____

The accountant has sent a memo requesting the following information for completing tax records. Remember that computer equipment has *CP* as the first two characters of the Item Code.

a.   The value of all computer equipment leased during 1991 _____; purchased during 1991 _____. The total value of computer equipment purchased and leased during 1991. (Add the Cost fields.) _____

b.   The value of all computer equipment leased during 1992 _____; purchased during 1992 _____. The total value of computer equipment purchased and leased during 1992. _____

Changing a Service Vendor

Name _____   Date _____

Section _____   Evaluation _____

A memo from the office has been received indicating that the service vendor for the electronic typewriters has been changed from Best Key Service to TriState Service. Update all electronic typewriter records to show this change. Electronic typewriters are identified with the code *TY*.

QUANTUM CORPORATION
INVENTORY FILE

EXERCISE 94

Printing a Report to List Service Vendors

Name _____ Date _____

Section _____ Evaluation _____

The sales director wants a report showing all equipment in that department and the service vendor for each. Title the report *Office Equipment and Service Vendors*. Sort alphabetically by service vendor. In the report, include data for the Item Code and Name, Service Vendor, Expiration Date, and Serial Number fields.

EXERCISE 95

Revising an Expiration Date

Name _____ Date _____

Section _____ Evaluation _____

TriState Service has offered a price reduction for a new service contract on all electronic typewriters, and Quantum management has chosen to accept the offer. The office manager has phoned to tell you that the new service contracts have been purchased for the electronic typewriters. The new contracts will expire 6 months from the expiration date currently shown in each of the records. Update all the electronic typewriter records by adding 6 to the month in the Expir. Date field. If the total is more than 12, subtract 12 from the total. The Item Code prefix for the typewriters is *TY*.

Producing a Graph or Summary Report

Name _____   Date _____

Section _____   Evaluation _____

The president of the company will be making a presentation to the stockholders on the assets of the company. As a part of that presentation, he would like to have a graph showing the distribution of the dollar value of the inventory by department.

If your database software has graphics capability (dBASE III+ can produce a bar graph and Lotus can produce a variety of types of graphs), produce the graph.

If you cannot produce the graph, produce a summary report giving the total value of the equipment in each department.

Note: Quantum has three departments, so your report will contain only three lines. The appropriate fields for this report are the Department and Cost fields.

Relating Equipment to Employees of Quantum

Name _____   Date _____

Section _____   Evaluation _____

You have been asked to provide the human resources manager with the names of all employees who have departmental access to the copier PC02 so that a memo can be sent out about a change in policy for using that machine. (*Hint:* This list will contain employees in the administration and research department where the copiers are kept.)

_____   _____   _____

_____   _____   _____

_____   _____   _____

_____   _____   _____

QUANTUM CORPORATION
INVENTORY FILE

EXERCISE 98

Preparing a Vendor Report

Name _____ Date _____

Section _____ Evaluation _____

Interstate Lines and Venus Repair have sent letters recently indicating an increase in their service contract prices. Because Quantum is getting ready to negotiate new service contracts with these vendors, the accountant has asked for a list of all equipment serviced by them. Do a primary sort by Service Vendor and a secondary sort by Item Code. Create an appropriate title and columnar headings for the report. Include the Item Code and Name, Purchased/Leased, Expiration Date, Service Vendor, and Last Service Date fields.

EXERCISE 99

Answering Inquiries

Name _____ Date _____

Section _____ Evaluation _____

TriState Service phoned to inform Quantum that Silktype typewriters with the serial numbers 0033333ØE and 4633386 need to have a defective part replaced. Send the following information to the administrative assistant in the administration department.

a. In which department is each of the typewriters located?

Serial number 0033333ØE—Dept: _____

Serial number 4633386—Dept: _____

b. When was each of these typewriters purchased?

Serial number 0033333ØE—Date Purchased? _____

Serial number 4633386—Date Purchased? _____

EXERCISE 100

Creating a Formal Printout

Name _____ Date _____

Section _____ Evaluation _____

The comptroller is preparing a budget for the company and needs data about monthly service/maintenance costs. To help with this task, create a report showing all equipment for which a monthly amount is paid. This will include all leased equipment and all equipment for which a service charge is paid. The report should show the item code, item name, whether it is purchased/leased, the lease amount where applicable, and the monthly service/maintenance fee where applicable. Include a total column to show the total monthly amounts paid for each item (that is, the lease cost + the service fee). Also include a column to show the yearly cost of each item. Index by department. At the department break, show a count by department and totals of each dollar amount. Show a final count of all items and a final total for each dollar amount at the end of the report. Create an appropriate report title and columnar headings.

EXERCISE 101

Test – Quantum Corporation's Inventory File

Your instructor will give you the test for this unit.

QUANTUM CORPORATION-EQUIPMENT INVENTORY LIST

ITEM CODE	ITEM NAME	DEPT	DATE P/L	P/L	EXPIR. DATE	SERIAL NO.	COST	SERVICE VENDOR	LAST SERVICE DATE	MANUFACTURER
AM01	Answering Machine	Sales	31-Mar-90	P	01-Jun	97A0109	295.00	Ace Machine Service	30-Jun-91	Teleco
CP01	Computer Modem	Admin.	01-Jul-90	L	01-Jul	M099437C	1550.00	Interstate Lines	31-Jul-91	Telmode
CP02	Computer Processor	Admin.	01-Jul-91	L	01-Jul	PCC847629	17225.00	City Computer Repair	20-Jan-92	Digiquip
CP03	Dot Matrix Printer	Admin.	01-Jul-91	P	01-Jul	M665784	7100.00	City Computer Repair	04-Jan-91	Deltacorp
CP04	Laser Printer	Admin.	01-Jul-90	P	01-Jul	L694300A	3995.00	City Computer Repair	01-Dec-91	Deltacorp
CP05	Computer Terminal	Admin.	01-Jul-91	L	01-Jul	T699784	2995.00	City Computer Repair	01-Aug-92	Digiquip
CP06	Computer Terminal	Admin.	01-Jul-91	L	01-Jul	T699788	2990.00	City Computer Repair	01-Jul-92	Digiquip
CP07	Computer Terminal	Research	01-Jul-90	L	01-Jul	T66986	3225.00	City Computer Repair	01-Jul-92	Digiquip
CP08	Computer Terminal	Research	01-Jul-90	L	01-Jul	T669876	3225.00	City Computer Repair	01-Jul-92	Digiquip
CP09	Computer Terminal	Research	01-Jul-90	L	01-Jul	T669881	3225.00	City Computer Repair	18-Feb-92	Digiquip
CP10	Line Printer	Sales	01-Jul-91	L	01-Jul	94ZTX449	15900.00	City Computer Repair	24-Jun-92	Deltacorp
CP11	Computer Terminal	Sales	01-Aug-92	L	01-Aug	T7778436	1200.00	City Computer Repair	20-Mar-92	Digiquip
DM01	Dictating Machine	Research	15-Nov-90	P	01-Feb	99870600	485.00	Venus Repair	03-Jul-91	Echo
DM02	Dictating Machine	Sales	15-Nov-90	P	01-Feb	6694211	485.00	Venus Repair	03-Jul-91	Echo
EC01	Electronic Calculator	Research	10-Jan-91	P	01-Mar	Z7104BB	425.00	Supra Machine Repair	19-Apr-91	E Z Key
EC02	Electronic Calculator	Admin.	01-Jul-91	P	01-Oct	Z7625BB	425.00	Supra Machine Repair	16-Mar-92	E Z Key
EC03	Electronic Calculator	Research	15-Jan-91	P	01-Jan	549000C	350.00	Supra Machine Repair	20-Jun-91	Electrocom
EC04	Electronic Calculator	Sales	15-Jan-90	P	01-Dec	669113C	350.00	Supra Machine Repair	20-Jun-91	Electrocom
AD01	Adding Machine	Admin.	01-Jun-89	P	01-Jan	D00066943	225.00	Best Key Service	13-Sep-91	Digiquip
PC01	Plain Paper Copier	Admin.	01-Jan-87	P	01-Apr	448M2	300.00	Venus Repair	15-Dec-92	Stevens
PC02	Plain Paper Copier	Research	18-Sep-92	P	01-Sep	128894C	3775.00	Venus Repair	01-Oct-92	Emperor
PR01	Check Protector	Admin.	01-May-91	P	01-May	P66849	150.00	Venus Repair	18-Mar-92	Checkpro
TY01	Electronic Typewriter	Admin.	30-Jun-91	P	01-Jun	4886A43	680.00	Best Key Service	27-Sep-92	Silktype
TY02	Electronic Typewriter	Research	30-Jun-91	P	01-Jun	9846BB2	680.00	Best Key Service	24-Jul-91	Silktype
TY03	Electronic Typewriter	Sales	15-Aug-90	P	01-Jan	60009988E	750.00	Best Key Service	16-Jan-91	Horizon
TY04	Electronic Typewriter	Admin.	01-Nov-93	P	01-Nov	00333330E	799.00	Best Key Service	28-Oct-93	Horizon
TY05	Electronic Typewriter	Sales	19-May-93	P	01-Nov	4633386	1290.00	Best Key Service	19-May-93	Silktype
TY06	Electronic Typewriter	Research	19-May-93	P	01-Nov	7684355	1290.00	Best Key Service	15-Nov-93	Silktype

Tutorial

UNIT I

Exercise 3–Creating the File

Help for dBASE Users

To access dBASE III+, at the system prompt key dBASE, and tap <Enter>. Tap <Enter> again to get past the license agreement. (This will bring you to the dBASE ASSIST menu system, also referred to as the *ASSISTANT*.) You will see a set of commands across the top of the monitor. These are menu choices. Since you are preparing to create a new database file, choose CREATE by tapping the Right Arrow key once. A drop-down menu appears giving you the choices for CREATE. What we are creating is a database file and that choice is already highlighted so you only need to tap <Enter>. Next, you must select the letter of the drive where your data disk is located. If you will be saving your work on Drive A, use the Up Arrow key to highlight the letter *A*. Likewise, if you will be saving your work on Drive B, use the Arrow keys to highlight the letter *B*. Once your data drive has been selected, tap the enter key. You have a prompt displayed asking you to name the database you are creating. Key a filename consisting of no more than eight characters. For this database, let's name this file **FAUNTERO.** After keying in the filename, tap <Enter>. A new screen appears where you will enter the field names for your database structure. Your cursor is resting at the position to enter the first field name. Tap the Caps Lock key so all of your field names are entered in capital letters. Field names may be up to ten characters long and may not contain blank spaces. If you wish to use more than one word for a field name, it must be connected with an underscore character. Key the field information as follows:

1. Key **ACCOUNT_NO**   The cursor automatically jumps to the next position because the highlighted area was completely filled with the name of the field.

2. <Enter>   Even though the account number consists of numbers, we treat it as a character field because we do not do arithmetic functions with an account number. Because the default format is set for a character field, simply tapping <Enter> confirms the default.

3. Key **5**   This is the width (length) of the ACCOUNT_NO field.

4. <Enter>   Note that decimals cannot be set in a
   <Enter>   character field.

The cursor is now in the row for field number two. (From now on, you will be given keystrokes without an explanation unless it is a new procedure.)

5. Key **NAME**   The field name did not fill up the 10 spaces so

6. <Enter>   you must tap <Enter> to move to the right.

7. <Enter>   This is a character field so no change is needed.

8. Key **28**

9. <Enter>

10. Key **INDEX_NAME**

11. <Enter>

12. Key **28**

13. <Enter>

14. Key **ADDRESS**

15. <Enter>

16. <Enter>

17. Key **25**

18. <Enter>

19. Key **CITY**

20. <Enter>

21. <Enter>

22. Key **20**

23. <Enter>

24. Key **STATE**

25. <Enter>

26. <Enter>

27. Key **2**

28. <Enter>

29. Key **ZIP**

30. <Enter>

31. <Enter>

32. Key **5**

33. <Enter>

34. Key **CREDIT_RAT**

35. Key **N**

36. Key **1**

37. <Enter>

38. Key **0**

39. <Enter>

40. Key **CREDIT_LMT**

41. Key **N**

42. Key **4**

43. <Enter>

44. Key **0**

45. <Enter>

46. Key **BALANCEDUE**

47. Key **N**

48. Key **7**

49. <Enter>

50. Key **2**

51. <Enter>

The cursor is now in the row for field 11. Because there are no more fields, tap <Enter> again to stop entering field names. Notice the message at the bottom of the monitor prompting you to tap <Enter> to confirm your choices. Read the monitor to be sure field names and their attributes are correct. If everything is correct, tap <Enter> to accept the new database structure. If you see an error, tap any key before making a change. Then use your arrow keys to move to the error. Make the change.

When you are satisfied that your database structure is correct, tap <Enter> repeatedly until you again see the message **Press Enter to Continue,** then tap <Enter> again to confirm your choices. Another prompt will appear at the bottom of the monitor asking you if you would like to input records now. If you are ready to do Exercise 4 and enter the data, key **Y.** If you must wait until later, key **N.**

Help for Lotus Users

1. Load Lotus 1-2-3 by keying **123** at the system prompt.

2. To access the main menu, tap /.

3. When a command is needed, tap the capitalized letter or use an Arrow key to highlight the command and then tap <Enter>. For example, to see the menu and use the **File** command, simply tap **/F.** To remove the menu from the monitor, tap <Esc>. You do not need to tap <Shift> to key the letters of commands.

4. Change the default drive so that your work will be saved to your data disk. Tap </, File, Directory, A:> (or <B:>) <Enter>. Repeat this procedure each time you begin a Lotus session.

5. With the cell pointer located in cell A1, key **^ACCOUNT,** tap the Down Arrow once, key **^NO.,** <Enter>. (The ^ centers the label in the column.) Change the width of the column to 7; tap /Worksheet, Column, Set-width, 7 <Enter>.

6. Tap the Right Arrow key once, key **^NAME** <Enter>.

7. Change width of the column to 29 as you did above.

8. Tap the Right Arrow key, key **^INDEXED NAME** <Enter>.

9. Change width of the column to 29.

10. Tap the Right Arrow key, key **^ADDRESS** <Enter>.

11. Change the width of the column to 26.

12. Tap the Right Arrow key, key **^CITY** <Enter>.

13. Change the width of the column to 20.

14. Tap the Right Arrow key, key **^STATE** <Enter>.

15. Change the width of the column to 5.

16. Tap the Right Arrow key, key **^ZIP** <Enter>.

17. Change the width of the column to 6.

18. Tap the Right Arrow key, the Up Arrow key, key **^CREDIT** <Down Arrow>, key **^RATING** <Enter>.

19. Change the width of the column to 10.

20. Tap <Right Arrow>, <Up Arrow>, key **^CREDIT** <Down Arrow>, key **^LIMIT** <Enter>.

21. Change the width of the column to 10.

22. Tap <Right Arrow>, <Up Arrow>, key **^BALANCE** <Down Arrow>, key **^DUE** <Enter>. Change the width of the column to 10.

23. Format the Balance Due column for dollars and cents. With the cell pointer in cell J3, tap /, Range, Format, Fixed, <Enter>, Down Arrow key to cell J42, <Enter>.

If you do not have time to continue the next exercise, save this part of the worksheet. Tap /, File, Save, enter a filename up to eight characters long, <Enter>. To exit 1-2-3, tap /, Quit, Yes.

Exercise 4–Keying Data From Forms 001 Through 036

Help for dBASE Users

1. If you were interrupted after Exercise 3, load dBASE III+.

2. **SET UP** is highlighted and **DATABASE** FILE is highlighted <Enter>.

3. Highlight the letter of the drive of your data disk.

4. <Enter>

5. The name of our previously created file, **FAUNTERO.DBF,** should be highlighted. If it is not, highlight it by using the Arrow keys.

6. <Enter>

7. Key **N** (to answer the question **Is the file indexed? [Y/N]**)

8. Tap the Right Arrow key twice to highlight **UPDATE.** The drop-down menu appears with the word **APPEND** highlighted.

9. <Enter>

You are now ready to enter data. The cursor is in the highlighted area to enter the ACCOUNT_NO.

10. Key the 5-digit number. A bell will sound, unless it has been turned off, and the cursor will jump to the next field.

11. Key the name.

12. <Enter>

13. Tap <Caps Lock>.

14. Key the indexed name.

15. Tap <Caps Lock>.

16. <Enter>

17. Key the address.

18. <Enter>

19. Key the city.

20. <Enter>

21. Key the state.

22. Key the ZIP Code.

23. Key the credit rating.

24. Key the credit limit.

25. <Enter> if necessary.

26. Key the balance due.

27. The screen scrolls (information moves up) so you may enter data for the next record. Continue entering all the records for this exercise. When you have finished entering the data, hold down the Control key and tap the End key (**Control/End**). This will save the data and take you back to the **ASSISTANT** screen.

Help for Lotus Users

1. Load Lotus 1-2-3.

2. If you are beginning a new session, retrieve the file created in Exercise 3. Remember to change the default drive as in Exercise 3. Tap /, File, Retrieve, highlight the filename, <Enter>.

3. Position the cell pointer on cell A3.

4. Begin keying the information from form 001. Key an apostrophe before the numeric data that is to be considered as character data. The keystrokes for the first form are as follows:

Key '**10934** <Right Arrow>, key **Douglas J. Hill** <Right Arrow>, key **HILL DOUGLAS J** <Right Arrow>, key '**245 1st Street NE** <Right Arrow>, key **Louisville** <Right Arrow>, key **KY** <Right Arrow>, key '**40243** <Right Arrow>, key **2** <Right Arrow>, key **500** <Right Arrow>, key **100**. Tap the Down Arrow once, and then hold down the Shift key and tap the Tab key twice to begin the next line of data. Key forms 2 through 36 using the same procedure.

5. When you are finished entering records, save the file as above, but this time you will see a prompt asking you whether to **Cancel, Replace,** or **Backup.** Choose **Replace** by keying an **R** or tapping <Right Arrow> once and then <Enter>. You would choose

Cancel only when you wish to stop the saving operation.

Exercise 5–Listing Customer Names and Account Numbers

Help for dBASE Users

1. Open the **FAUNTERO** database file.

2. Sort the file on indexed name as follows: Tap the Right Arrow key to highlight the menu choice **ORGANIZE** or tap **O** for **ORGANIZE**.

3. From the drop-down menu, use the Down Arrow key to highlight the word **SORT**. <Enter>

4. Tap the Down Arrow key twice to highlight **INDEX_NAME** <Enter>.

5. Tap either the Left or Right Arrow key once.

(The drive of your data disk should be highlighted.) <Enter>

6. Enter a new filename, such as **CUSTOMER**, for the sorted file. Key **CUSTOMER** <Enter>

7. Wait for the records to be sorted. When **Press any key to continue work in ASSIST** appears, tap a key.

8. Make the **CUSTOMER** file active by highlighting the *SET UP* option <Enter>.

9. The drive where your data disk is located should be highlighted <Enter>.

10. Tap the Down Arrow key until the **CUSTOMER.DBF** file is highlighted <Enter>.

11. Key **N** (The file is not indexed)

12. Tap **R** for the menu option **RETRIEVE**.

13. **LIST** should be highlighted <Enter>.

14. Tap the Down Arrow key twice to highlight **CONSTRUCT A FIELD LIST** <Enter>.

15. <Enter> To accept **ACCOUNT_NO**.

16. <Enter> To accept **NAME**.

17. Tap <Right Arrow> once to leave this menu.

18. Tap <Up Arrow> twice to select **EXECUTE THE COMMAND** <Enter>.

19. Answer the question of whether or not you want the output sent to the printer. It is suggested that you answer *N* the first time so the output is sent to the monitor for viewing to ensure that your output is correct. If you want to send the output to the printer, answer with a *Y*.

Help for Lotus Users

1. Load the file that was created in Exercise 4.

2. When sorting the spreadsheet, do not save it unless you give the sorted version a new filename. To sort the spreadsheet, place the cell pointer in cell A3. (The field names, rows 1 and 2, are not part of the sort range since they are not to be sorted with the

customer information). Tap /, Data, Sort, Data-Range, . (the period is to lock in the beginning of the range), tap <Tab> twice, <PgDn> once, and <Down Arrow> 15 times to "paint" or highlight all the information you entered in Exercise 4. (The data-range should be A3..J38) Tap <Enter>, <Primary-key>, <Right Arrow> twice to C3, <Enter>, key **A** for Ascending-order, <Enter>, key **G** for **GO.**

3. Tap the Home key.

4. Tap /, Print, Printer, Range, A1..B38, <Enter>, Go. After printing is completed, tap Quit.

Exercise 6–Proofreading Your Listing

Help for dBASE Users

If corrections need to be made, follow these steps:

1. Open the **FAUNTERO** database file if it is not already open.

2. Tap **U** for **UPDATE.**

3. Tap <Down Arrow> to highlight **BROWSE** <Enter>.

4. Scroll the cursor through the list of customers until the highlight is on the customer you are looking for.

5. Tap <Control> and the Left or Right Arrow key to move to the field that is to be changed. The monitor is not wide enough for all of the information to be displayed at one time. Tapping <Control> and the Left or Right Arrow key will scroll information left and right.

6. Tap <Control/Y> to delete the incorrect data.

7. Key the new data.

8. Continue to search for and update other records that contain errors.

9. Tap <Control/End> when you have corrected all errors.

Help for Lotus Users

If errors are found, look through the spreadsheet for the customer, use the Arrow keys to highlight the error. Re-key the information or tap <F2> to edit the existing entry.

Exercise 7–Helping the Accountant

Help for dBASE Users

7a.

1. Tap **R** for **RETRIEVE.**

2. <Enter> to accept **LIST.**

3. Tap <Down Arrow> to **CONSTRUCT A FIELD LIST** <Enter>.

4. <Enter> to accept **ACCOUNT_NO.**

5. Tap <Down Arrow> until **CITY** is highlighted <Enter>.

6. Tap <Down Arrow> until **STATE** is highlighted <Enter>.

7. Tap <Right Arrow> once.

8. **BUILD A SEARCH CONDITION** is highlighted <Enter>.

9. Tap <Down Arrow> four times until **CITY** is highlighted <Enter>.

10. A pop-up menu appears giving you operational choices. <Enter> to accept **EQUAL TO.**

11. Key **LOUISVILLE** <Enter>.

12. Tap <Down Arrow> until **COMBINE WITH AND** is highlighted <Enter>.

13. Tap <Down Arrow> until **STATE** is highlighted <Enter> <Enter>.

14. Key **KY. NO MORE CONDITIONS** is highlighted. <Enter>

15. <Up Arrow> to highlight **EXECUTE THE COMMAND** <Enter>.

16. Decide whether to send output to the printer or to the monitor.

7b.

1. Highlight **RETRIEVE** <Enter>.

2. Tap <Down Arrow> twice to highlight **CONSTRUCT A FIELD LIST** <Enter> <Enter>.

3. Tap <Down Arrow> to highlight **BALANCEDUE** <Enter>.

4. Tap <Right Arrow> to leave this menu.

5. **BUILD A SEARCH CONDITION** is highlighted <Enter>.

6. Tap <Down Arrow> 9 times to highlight **BALANCEDUE** <Enter>.

7. Tao <Down Arrow> three times to highlight **GREATER THAN** <Enter>.

8. Key **2000.00** <Enter>.

9. <Enter> to accept **NO MORE CONDITIONS.**

10. Tap <Up Arrow> twice to highlight **EXECUTE THE COMMAND** <Enter>.

11. Decide whether to send the output to the printer or to the monitor.

7c.

1. Tap **R** for **RETRIEVE** <Enter>.

2. Tap <Down Arrow> until **CONSTRUCT A FIELD LIST** is highlighted <Enter>.

3. <Enter> to accept **ACCOUNT_NO.**

4. Tap <Down Arrow> until **CREDIT_RAT** is highlighted <Enter>.

5. Tap <Down Arrow> until **BALANCEDUE** is highlighted <Enter>.

6. Tap <Right Arrow> once. <Enter> to accept **BUILD A SEARCH CONDITION.**

7. Tap <Down Arrow> until **CREDIT_RAT** is highlighted <Enter>.

8. <Enter> to choose **EQUAL TO.**

9. Key **3.**

10. Tap <Down Arrow> once to highlight **COMBINE WITH AND** <Enter>.

11. Tap <Down Arrow> until **BALANCEDUE** is highlighted <Enter>.

12. Tap <Down Arrow> until **GREATER THAN** is highlighted <Enter>.

13. Key **500** <Enter>.

14. <Enter> to choose **NO MORE CONDITIONS.**

15. Tap <Up Arrow> until *EXECUTE THE COMMAND* is highlighted <Enter>.

16. Decide whether to send the output to the printer or to the monitor.

7d.

1. **RETRIEVE.**

2. **LIST** <Enter>.

3. **CONSTRUCT A FIELD LIST** <Enter>.

4. Highlight **STATE** <Enter>.

5. <Right Arrow> once.

6. **BUILD A SEARCH CONDITION** <Enter>.

7. Highlight **STATE** <Enter>.

8. **EQUAL TO** <Enter>.

9. Key **OH.**

10. **NO MORE CONDITIONS.**

11. **EXECUTE THE COMMAND.**

12. Decide whether to send the output to the printer or to the monitor.

Repeat the above steps for the remainder of the exercise.

Help for Lotus Users

7a.

1. Sort the spreadsheet on the **CITY** field as follows: Position the cell pointer on cell A3, /, Data, Sort, Data-Range, (this should already be set **A3..J38**), <Enter>, Primary-key, position cell pointer on cell E3 or key <E3>, <Enter>, A, <Enter>, **Go.**

2. Use the Right Arrow to move to the CITY column, tap <Down Arrow> until you find the city you are looking for. Use Left Arrow key to move to the **ACCOUNT NO.** column to retrieve the information asked for. Rows 23 through 35 contain the information for this exercise if your spreadsheet was sorted correctly.

7b.

Sort the spreadsheet on **BALANCE DUE.** Refer to 7a. Use the Arrow keys to locate the information. Rows 36

through 38 contain the correct information for this exercise if your spreadsheet was sorted correctly in ascending order.

7c.

Sort the spreadsheet on two keys. Perform the same steps as in 7a, except after keying the Primary-key of credit rating, choose Secondary-key of balance due in ascending order: /, Data, Sort, Data-Range, <Enter>, Primary-key, <H3>, (or cursor to the first entry in the Credit Rating column), <Enter>, A, <Enter>, Secondary-key, <J3>, (or cursor to the first entry in the Balance Due column), <Enter>, **A,** <Enter>, **Go.** Use Arrow keys to locate information. Columns 37 and 38 contain the correct information if both sorts were in ascending order.

7d.

Sort the spreadsheet on **STATE.** Use the Arrow keys to locate the information.

Exercise 8—Finding the Customers

Help for dBASE Users

1. **RETRIEVE.**

2. **LIST** <Enter>.

3. **CONSTRUCT A FIELD LIST** <Enter>.

4. Highlight **STATE** <Enter>.

5. <Right Arrow> once.

6. **BUILD A SEARCH CONDITION** <Enter>.

7. Highlight **STATE** <Enter>.

8. **NOT EQUAL TO** <Enter>.

9. Key **KY.**

10. **COMBINE WITH AND** <Enter>.

11. Highlight **STATE** <Enter>.

12. **NOT EQUAL TO** <Enter>.

13. Key **OH.**

14. **COMBINE WITH AND** <Enter>.

15. Highlight **STATE** <Enter>.

16. **NOT EQUAL TO** <Enter>.

17. Key **IN.**

18. **NO MORE CONDITIONS** <Enter>.

19. **EXECUTE THE COMMAND.**

20. Decide whether to send the output to the screen or to the monitor.

Help for Lotus Users

With the spreadsheet sorted on State, use the Arrow keys to locate the information.

Exercise 9–Adding New Customers

Help for dBASE Users

Be sure to use the original database file when

updating.

1. Open the FAUNTERO database.

2. **UPDATE.**

3. **APPEND** <Enter>.

4. Enter records as you did in Exercise 4.

Note: The status line at the bottom of the monitor indicates what mode you are in (**APPEND**), which drive is the default (**A**), the name of the active database (**FAUNTERO**). **REC:** stands for record, **EOF** stands for end of file, and if **CAPS** is at the end of this line, it means that the Caps Lock key is on.

Help for Lotus Users

1. Load the original file.

2. Position the cell pointer on cell A39.

3. Enter the new customers just as you did in Exercise 4.

4. Save the file under the original filename.

Exercise 10–Updating Records

Help for dBASE Users

You may have learned how to make changes to a file in Exercise 6. The following steps are a different method of updating. You may use either method.

1. Open the **FAUNTERO** database file.

2. Highlight **UPDATE.**

3. Tap <Down Arrow> until **BROWSE** is highlighted <Enter>.

4. Scroll the cursor through the list of customers until the highlight is on the one you are looking for.

5. Tap <ESC>.

6. <Up Arrow> twice to choose **EDIT** <Enter>.

7. Tap <Down Arrow> until the cursor is in the field that is to be changed.

8. Tap <Control/Y> to delete the original information in that field.

9. Key the new data.

10. Tap <Control/End> to exit and save the changes.

Try both the above method and that described in Exercise 6. Decide which method you prefer.

Help for Lotus Users

1. /, Range, Search, A3..A38, <Enter>, key **26261**, <Enter>, Labels, Find, Quit. Press <Right Arrow> three times, /, Range, Erase, <Enter>.

2. Key the new address.

3. Search for the other records in a similar way, being careful to enter the correct **"Range to search for:"** and **"String to search for:"** information.

4. Save the updated file under the original filename.

Exercise 11–Printing Mailing Labels

Help for dBASE Users

1. Open the **FAUNTERO** database.

2. Sort the file on ZIP code. Refer to Exercise 5 for help on sorting.

3. After sorting, open the sorted file.

4. Tap the Right Arrow key once to choose **CREATE** from the menu.

5. Tap <Down Arrow> six times to select **LABELS** <Enter> <Enter>.

6. Key a filename for the label format <Enter>.

7. A menu with predefined options for the labels should be on the monitor. Check with your instructor to see what type of labels you will be using. (The predefined setting is for 3" x 15/16" x 1 labels. The 3" is the width of the label, the 15/16" is the height of the label, and the 1 is the number of labels across the page.) <Enter>.

8. Tap <Right Arrow> once to highlight the **CONTENTS** option <Enter> <F10>.

9. Tap <Down Arrow> once to choose **NAME** <Enter> <Enter>.

10. Tap <Down Arrow> once to line 2 <Enter> <F10>.

11. Tap <Down Arrow> three times to **ADDRESS** <Enter> <Enter>.

12. Tap <Down Arrow> once to line 3 <Enter> <F10>.

13. Tap <Down Arrow> 4 times to **CITY** <Enter>.

14. Key , <F10>.

15. Tap <Down Arrow> 5 times to **STATE** <Enter>.

16. Key , <F10>.

17. Tap <Down Arrow> 6 times to **ZIP** <Enter> <Enter>.

18. Tap <Right Arrow> once to highlight **EXIT. SAVE** will also be highlighted <Enter>.

19. Highlight **RETRIEVE.**

20. Tap <Down Arrow> until **LABEL** is highlighted <Enter> <Enter>.

21. Highlight the filename that you just created for the label format <Enter>.

22. Build search conditions for locating the customers as you did in Exercise 7.

23. Print the labels.

Help for Lotus Users

Lotus, which is a spreadsheet, is typically not used for the production of mailing labels in small office operations. However, it can be done through the use of macros. Data from a Lotus file can also be imported into a word processing software package for printing mailing labels. Students using Lotus should prepare this exercise up to the point of printing mailing labels. Sort the spreadsheet on **ZIP** as the primary key and **CITY** as the secondary key.

Exercise 12–Printing a Customer Report

Help for dBASE Users

1. Open the **FAUNTERO** database and sort it on the account number.

2. Open the sorted file.

3. Highlight **CREATE**.

4. Tap <Down Arrow> until **REPORT** is highlighted.

5. Key a filename for the report format <Enter>.

6. <Enter> to input a page title.

7. Key **CUSTOMER REPORT WITH BALANCES GREATER THAN $1000** <Control/End>.

8. *Tap <Right Arrow> twice to highlight **COLUMNS** <Enter> <F10>.

9. <Enter> to accept **ACCOUNT_NO**.

10. Tap <Down Arrow> once to highlight **HEADING** <Enter>.

11. Key **ACCOUNT** <Enter>.

12. Key **NUMBER** <Control/End>.

13. Tap <Down Arrow> three times to highlight **TOTAL THIS COLUMN** <Enter> to change the default to **NO**.

14. **Tap <PgDn> to fill in information for next column. Repeat steps * through ** for the remainder of the fields that are to be included in the report. When the last column has been set up, tap <Right Arrow> once to highlight **EXIT**. With **SAVE** also highlighted, tap <Enter>.

15. Refer to Exercise 11 for retrieving the report format. It is very similar to a label format.

Help for Lotus Users

1. Load the **FAUNTERO** worksheet.

2. Tap /, Worksheet, Delete, Column, C1..G1, <Enter>.

3. Sort the worksheet on **BALANCE DUE**.

4. Delete all of the rows A3 through A33 by tapping /, Worksheet, Delete, Row, A3..A33, <Enter>. (Or paint the range of rows to be deleted.) Print the report.

Exercise 13–Answering Phone Inquiries

Help for dBASE Users

This exercise will be easier if you use the **CUSTOMER** database file.

1. Highlight **UPDATE**.

2. <Down Arrow> to select **BROWSE** <Enter>.

3. Search the customer list, make the change, and retrieve the information requested.

Help for Lotus Users

13a.

/, Range, Search, C3..C38, <Enter>, <Esc>, key **HAL**, <Enter>, Labels, Find, Next, Quit. Press <Right Arrow> five times. (You will select **NEXT** only if the incorrect **HAL** is found). Answer the question.

13b.

<Home>. /, Range, Search, C3..C38, <Enter>, <Esc>, key **MANUAL**, <Enter>, Labels, Find, Quit. Tap <Right Arrow> seven times. Answer the question.

13c.

<Home>. /, Range, Search, C3..C38, <Enter>, <Esc>, key **ALLEN**, <Enter>, Labels, Find, Quit. Tap <Right Arrow> seven times, tap <F2>, key **+159**, <Enter>. Answer the question.

13d.

1. <Home>. /, Range, Search, C3..C38, <Enter>, <Esc>, key **STJAMES**, <Enter>, Labels, Find, Quit. Tap <Left Arrow> twice. Answer the question.

2. <Home>. /, Range, Search, C3..C38, <Enter>, <Esc>, key **FULLER**, <Enter>, Labels, Find, Quit. Tap <Right Arrow> to find the address.

Exercise 14–Deleting Records

Help for dBASE Users

1. Open the **FAUNTERO** database.

2. Tap <Right Arrow> twice to highlight **UPDATE**.

3. Tap <Down Arrow> three times to highlight **BROWSE** <Enter>.

4. Search the customer list to find the record you wish to delete.

5. With that record highlighted, tap <**CONTROL U**>. (The record still appears on the monitor. It has just been marked for deletion.)

6. Find the other records to delete and mark them in the same manner <Control/End>.

7. Tap <Down Arrow> four times to highlight **PACK**. (This option completely deletes the records previously marked for deletion.) <Enter> <Enter>.

Help for Lotus Users

1. Load the original file.

2. Find the record: <Home>. /, Range, Search, A3..A38, key **30272**, <Enter>, Labels, Find, Quit.

3. Delete the record: /, Worksheet, Delete, Row, <Enter>. (The cell pointer should be on the record to be deleted.)

4. Search for and delete the other records in a similar manner.

Exercise 15–Listing Paid-Up Customers

Help for dBASE Users

1. Open the **FAUNTERO** database file.

2. Sort the file on indexed name and then open the sorted file. (You may name the sorted file **CUSTOMER** as in Exercise 5. Key **Y** in response to the overwrite the file question.)

3. Refer to Exercises 11 and 12 to prepare this report.

4. Use **CUSTOMERS WITH A ZERO BALANCE** as the title.

5. The search condition will be BALANCEDUE = 0.

Help for Lotus Users

1. Sort on Balance Due and Indexed Name: /, Data, Sort, Data-range, A3..J38, <Enter>, Primary-key, **J3**, <Enter>, **A**, <Enter>, Secondary-key, **C3**, <Enter>, **A**, <Enter>, **Go**.

2. Print range A1 through C11.

Exercise 16–Checking Credit Limits

Help for dBASE Users

1. Open the **CUSTOMER** database file.

2. Refer to Exercises 11 and 12 to prepare this report.

3. Title the report *Customers with $500 credit limit and credit rating of one.*

4. The search condition is credit limit = **500** and credit rating = **1**.

Help for Lotus Users

1. Sort the spreadsheet to group the customers whose Credit Limit is $500 and Credit Rating is **1**.

2. Delete the fields that are not needed in the report.

3. Delete the customers that are not needed in the report.

4. Sort the remaining spreadsheet on Indexed Name.

5. Print the report.

Exercise 17–Modifying the Database Structure and Updating Records

Help for dBASE Users

17a.

1. Tap <M> for **MODIFY**. <Enter> to accept **DATABASE FILE**.

2. Tap <Down Arrow> six times to highlight **ZIP** <Enter> <Enter>.

3. <Control/y> to delete the contents.

4. Key **10** <Enter>.

5. <Control/End>.

17b.

Refer to Exercise 10.

Help for Lotus Users

17a.

Tap Right Arrow key to the **ZIP (G)** column. Widen the column by tapping /, Worksheet, Column, Set-width, 10, <Enter>.

17b.

Locate the records to be updated and make the changes as in Exercise 10. Save the spreadsheet.

Exercise 18–Adding More New Customers

Help for dBASE Users

Refer to Exercise 9.

Help for Lotus Users

Add new customers as you did in Exercise 9. Save the spreadsheet.

Exercise 19–Answering More Inquiries

Help for dBASE Users

Use the **BROWSE** mode to answer the questions.

Help for Lotus Users

Use **Search** to locate this information as you did in Exercise 13.

Exercise 20–Reporting Preferred Customers

Help for dBASE Users

1. Open the **FAUNTERO** database file.

2. Sort on **CITY**.

3. Open this sorted file.

4. When designing the report format, set left and right margins at zero.

5. Refer to Exercises 11 and 12 to prepare the report.

Help for Lotus Users

Sort the spreadsheet on **CREDIT LIMIT** as the primary key and **CITY** as the secondary key. Print the report.

UNIT II

Hints for Lotus Users

Selecting Data Meeting Certain Criteria

One of the best ways to select records meeting certain criteria with Lotus is to use the Data Query function. This is easiest to use if you first use /Range Name Create to define your Input, Criteria, and Output ranges.

Typically, your Input range will include your column headings and your entire database. Use /Range Name Create <Range Name> <Return> <Input range>. (*Hint:* With the cursor on the first cell in your database, press <dot> <END> followed by the Down Arrow. Then press <END> followed by the Right Arrow. This should highlight all entries unless you have some blank rows or columns.)

Next, use the /Copy function to copy the entire row with your field names to a cell several (at least 15) rows below your database. Then use /Range Name Create <Range Name> to name your Criteria range. The Criteria range should include the field name row plus an extra empty row below it in which you will place your search criteria.

Again use the /Copy function to copy the entire row of field names several rows below your Criteria range. Then /Range Name Create your Output range. This time only define the one row with the field names as your Output range. This way Lotus will use any number of rows it needs to list all the data extracted.

You can use the /Data Query function to Find, Extract, or Delete selected records. For reports and for many searches, you will want to Extract the selected records. First, type the search criteria below the appropriate fields in the Criteria range you named. Next, type /Data Query Input (Input range name—use the range name you created) <Return> Criteria (Criteria range name) <Return> Output (Output range name) <Return> Extract Quit. Now you can go to the Output area (use the F5 key and type in your Output range name) to view the data selected.

Printing Reports

Use the /Data Query function described above to extract the records needed for your report. When you do not wish to include all columns in your database in the report, exclude the unneeded ones with the /Worksheet Column Hide command. Print the report (specify your Output range name as the range to be printed) and then restore the hidden columns with /Worksheet Column Display <Return>.

Exercise 22–Creating the File

Help for dBASE Users

dBASE gives you a choice of using the **ASSIST** menu, which is menu-driven, or the "dot prompt," which is command-driven. The help for dBASE users given in Unit 1 was menu-oriented. As you become more familiar with dBASE, you will be able to perform many tasks more efficiently at the "dot prompt." You can easily toggle from the **ASSIST** menu to the dot prompt by tapping the ESCAPE key and from the dot prompt to the **ASSIST** menu by tapping the **F2** key.

Exercise 23–Inputting the Data From Forms 001 Through 028

Help for dBASE Users

Before you input the first record, ESCAPE to the dot prompt and key:

SET DATE ANSI

This will allow you to type the date in the format [*yy.mm.dd*] rather than in the default format [*mm/dd/yy*]. *You will need to repeat this command at the beginning of each session because this date format [yy.mm.dd] is not the default date format.*

Exercise 24–Listing the Entire File

Help for dBASE Users

In Unit I you created and used sorted files; however, it is usually more efficient to create and use index files. An index file contains pointers to records in the file currently in use. As long as indexed files are made active when the master file is opened, all changes made to the master file will automatically be made to the indexed file or files as well. This eliminates the need to switch from sorted files to the master file for updating records and then re-sorting the sorted files. To create and open an indexed file on last name field **(LNAME)**, key:

INDEX ON LNAME TO LNAME

You are creating an index file called **LNAME** (with the **TO LNAME** portion of the command). When you end a dBASE session and begin a new dBASE session, you must open the master file and the index file by keying:

USE EMPLOYEE INDEX LNAME

This command will list records in alphabetic order according to **LNAME.**

Help for Lotus Users

Refer to Exercise 5 in Unit I for sorting and listing.

Exercise 25–Searching the File

Help for dBASE Users

Item a. asks for names and dates of employment. You will need to create an index by the field **DOE** in order to see the record with the oldest date in this field (refer to the help hint in Exercise 24). You may limit the fields to be listed by keying:

LIST LNAME, FNAME, MINITIAL, DOE

Item b. asks for name and date of birth for employees whose birthday is in the current month. You may combine the fields you wish to list and the condition for listing records by keying:

LIST LNAME, FNAME, MINITIAL, DOB FOR MONTH(DOB) = "05"

This command, including the MONTH function, will search the **DOB** field for all records in which the month is equal to 05 (or the current month) even though the month is embedded in the middle of the field (yy.mm.dd).

Item c. asks for a total number of records meeting a condition rather than the contents of those records. The **COUNT** command will count and show the total number of records requested. Key at the dot prompt:

COUNT FOR WTYPE = "H"

The word **COUNT** is substituted for the word LIST in this application.

Item d. asks for more than one condition to be met. The **.AND.** and the **.OR.** allow you to combine multiple conditions for listing or counting records. The **.AND.** requires that both conditions be met in order to list or count the record; the **.OR.** lists or counts the record if either condition is met. Key at the dot prompt:

COUNT FOR MSTATUS = "S" .AND. WITHALLOW = 0

Note that you do not need quotes (" ") around the zero, because **WITHHOLDING ALLOWANCES** was defined as a numeric field when you created the file.

Help for Lotus Users

a. Sort on the DOE field.

b. One quick way to find these employees is to sort on the DOB field and to use the /Range Search command.

Exercise 26–Listing Hourly Employees in the Research Department

Help for dBASE Users

The words (**TO PRINT**) added to a **LIST** command will direct the data to the printer. Key at the dot prompt:

LIST LNAME, FNAME, MINITIAL, DOE FOR WTYPE = "H" .AND. DEPT = "Research" TO PRINT

Help for Lotus Users

Use the instructions to extract the hourly employees in the Research Dept. and to print the listing.

Exercise 27–Adding New Employees

Use the <END> Down Arrow to get to the next blank row for adding data quickly.

Exercise 30–Answering Inquiries

Help for dBASE Users

Remember the **DOB** field is defined as a date field; therefore, the DTOC function must be included in the command in order to search that field. Key at the dot prompt:

LIST FNAME, MINITIAL, LNAME, SSNO FOR DTOC (DOB) > "65.12.31"

Help for Lotus Users

Sort using the **DOB** field as the primary key in descending order and LNAME as the secondary field ascending.

EXERCISE 34–Deleting Records

Help for dBASE Users

To physically delete these records, key: **PACK** after you delete the records using the **DELETE** command.

Help for Lotus Users

Place the social security number in your Criteria field and use /Data Query <Delete> <Delete> for each record.

Exercise 37–Listing Research Department Employees

Help for dBASE Users

You will set the index to the indexed file you created earlier called **LNAME** in order to list the names in that order. Key at the dot prompt:

SET INDEX TO LNAME

Exercise 39–Reporting Employees By Department

Help for dBASE Users

To index by a primary and a secondary field, key at the dot prompt:

INDEX ON DEPT + LNAME TO DEPTNAME

The first field listed is the primary key and the second is the secondary key. Notice that the primary and secondary key fields are separated by a (+) symbol.

Exercise 40–Reporting the Sales Employees

Help for dBASE Users

After you create the report and the indexed file, you may list only employees in the sales department by keying at the dot prompt:

REPORT FORM SREPORT FOR DEPT = "Sales" TO PRINT
SREPORT is the name of the report.

Exercise 41–Changing Job Titles

Help for dBASE Users

You may use the **REPLACE** command to alter several records at once.

Key at the dot prompt:

REPLACE JTITLE WITH "Research Assoc." FOR JTITLE = "Research Asst."

Help for Lotus Users

Use /Range Search (range to search) Labels Replace (replacement string).

Exercise 44–Changing Wage Type

Help for dBASE Users

Use the following command at the dot prompt:

REPLACE WTYPE WITH "S" FOR JTITLE = "Research Assoc."

This will update all records at once that meet our standard.

UNIT III

Exercise 52–Creating a Custom Screen

Help for dBASE Users

Use your menu option **CREATE.** Then, choose the **FORMAT** option and follow the directions on each screen. Be sure to save the format or screen when you finish. You will need to set up the format when you open your file for use.

Exercise 54–Inputting Data From Forms 025 Through 056

Help for Lotus Users

If you are using the data diskette, you will need to retrieve the file for Unit III and fill in the indexed name field for each record.

EXERCISE 60–Preparing Mailing Labels for Wholesalers

Help for dBASE Users

Refer to the mailing label help given in Unit I.

Help for Lotus Users

Refer to Exercise 11 in Unit I.

Exercise 61–Finding the Researchers

Extract the proper data into your Output range and then sort the Output range.

Exercise 63–Searching for Clients in Los Angeles and Their Client Representatives

Help for dBASE Users

Key at the dot prompt:

Key These:	Explanation:
CLOSE DATABASES	(It is best to start with a clean slate.)
SELECT A	(This allows you to open your primary file, the file you are using most.)
USE CLIENT	(This opens the primary file—**CLIENT.**)
SELECT B	(This allows you to open the secondary files.)
USE EMPLOYEE INDEX LNAME	(This opens the secondary file—**EMPLOYEE,** and it must be indexed by the field each file shares in common. **LNAME** is the common field, and it is the name of the indexed file.)
SELECT A	(The primary file must be opened or made active again.)
SET RELATION LNAME INTO EMPLOYEE	(This establishes the TO relationship between the two files by a field, **LNAME.** Remember that the **LNAME** field must be identical in both files by its name, type, and width.)
GO TOP	(This will position the pointer to the top of the file in order to begin the relationship between the files.)
LIST NAME, LNAME, B->PHONE FOR CITY = "Los Angeles"	(The **B->PHONE** portion of the command tells dBASE to find the client representative phone numbers in the **EMPLOYEE** file, which was selected as file **B.**)

Help for Lotus Users

Lotus does not support relational database searches of this type.

Exercise 64–Reporting the Total Number of Clients Served by Each Client Representative

Help for dBASE Users

In order to obtain a count of clients for each client representative, you may use the **IMMEDIATE IF** function. When identifying the contents of a column while creating the report, use this phrase: IFF (LNAME > " ",1,1). This command will count each record even though the items are not identified as numeric.

Help for Lotus Users

Sort on client representative. Write down the client representatives' names.

The @DCOUNT function will count the number of records that meet a certain criterion. First you will need to identify an Input range, the Offset, and the Criterion range. The Input range will be the entire database, including the row with the field names. Use /Range Name Create to name the Input range. The Criterion range should be set up in a separate place and should contain a cell with the field name for the client representative with an empty cell below it. Assign the Name Create to name it. The offset represents the field (or column) from which you wish to count records. It is the number of columns away from the first column minus 1. The first column will be numbered **0**, the second column will be numbered **1**, the third column will be numbered **2**, etc. *Note:* you could use 0 as your offset since it represents the client number.

Go to the Criterion range. Below the field name, type in the first client representative's name.

Go to an empty cell at the bottom of your database and copy in the first client representative's name. This is for the report. Beside it type in the formula @DCOUNT(<Input range name>, <Offset>, <Criterion range name>). Then put the name of the second client representative in the criterion cell and in the report cell beneath the first client rep's name. /Copy the formula into the cell beside it. Repeat these steps until you have all the client reps' names and a count of all the clients served by that client rep.

UNIT IV

Exercise 79–Writing a Program/Macro

Help for dBASE Users

In this exercise you will write a simple program using the **MODIFY COMMAND** statement. Key at the dot prompt:

Key These:	Explanation:
MODIFY COMMAND SPROGRAM	This will allow you to enter the instructions for your program, called **SPROGRAM.**

On the next screen, you may key your instructions. Each line must be ended by tapping the **ENTER** key.

CLEAR	This will clear your screen before the output is displayed.
ACCEPT 'ENTER THE ITEMCODE YOU WANT DISPLAYED: TO CODE	This will allow you to input the Item Code of 'the record you want to be located. The Item Code you input will be held in a storage location called **CODE.**
LIST ICODE, INAME, SERIAL FOR ICODE = CODE	This will list the Item Code **(ICODE)** field, Item Name **(INAME)** field, and the Serial Number **(SERIAL)** field to be listed for the Item Code you name in the previous instruction.
RETURN	To end the program and save these lines depress <CONTROL> and tap **W.**

You may execute the program called **SPROGRAM** by keying: **DO SPROGRAM.**

Help for Lotus Users

When writing a macro, practice the operation you wish to perform. Write down all the keystrokes you used to make it work.

Refer to the list of macro commands given in your Lotus manual. You might use commands to accept a label entry from the keyboard for the Search criterion field name and the Search criterion. Then type in the keystrokes you wrote down. (Remember to precede all macro commands with an apostrophe (') to identify them as labels.)

Name your macro with a /Range Name Create. Macros are named with a backslash (\) and a single letter (for example: \M).

Exercise 83–Finding Equipment Needing Service

Help for dBASE Users

Refer to the help given for Exercise 25.

Exercise 85–Helping the Office Manager

Refer to the help given for Exercise 30.

Exercise 87–Altering the Database

Help for Lotus Users

To add fields, simply tab over to the next available column and enter your field name and data.

Exercise 89–Finding Equipment Value

Help for dBASE Users

dBASE will allow you to add the amounts in a field defined as **NUMERIC** by using the **SUM** command. To total the value of equipment in the administration department, key:

SUM COST FOR DEPT = "Admin."

Help for Lotus Users

Extract the data for each department into your Output field. Use the @SUM function to get the total value for each department.

Exercise 93–Changing a Service Vendor

Help for dBASE Users

Refer to the help given for Exercise 41.

Exercise 96–Producing a Graph or Summary Report

Help for Lotus Users

Producing a graph with Lotus is easy. You can sort your database on department and note the range of costs for each department. Go to an empty area in your spreadsheet and use @SUM to total each department's cost. Beside these totals type in the department name as a label for your graph. Type /Graph Type. The graph you wish to create could be a bar or pie graph. If you wish to create a bar graph, type Bar; if you want a pie graph, type Pie. Select **X.** The range for your X-axis includes the columns with the department name labels which you typed beside your department totals. Then select **A, B,** and **C.** The ranges for **A, B,** and **C** are all the cells with the totals. Next select **View.**

If you wish to print your graph, you must **SAVE** it and use the **Print Graph** disk.

Exercise 97–Relating Equipment to Employees of Quantum

Help for dBASE Users

Refer to the help given in Exercise 63.

Exercise 98–Preparing a Vendor Report

Help for dBASE Users

Refer to the help given in Exercise 39.

Appendix

Key to Indexing Database Names

Unit I

Exercise 2C, Optional Indexing Exercise, Page 10

HILL, DOUGLAS J
SHELTON WILLIAM EDWARD
VANHORN COLLEEN T
ZIMMERMAN JOSEPH J
ALSHAMMARI FALEH MOHAMMED
GREENSFELT STEVEN M
ALLEN JOEL P LT
WRIGHT PAUL LYNN
LABBIE JENNIFER LYNN
TAYLOR T DALTON
MCMICHAEL MARTIN G
MANUEL ROBERTO F
SMITH GEORGE W
HANCOCK PETER M
SANDERS JERON P
FULLER JAMES P
POPEK LEON W
PROSKE SARAH L
KIM CHEE WON
SHELLEY D SANDERS
ROTHBARRE SERENA K
STJAMES SANDRA T
KIMBELL CYNTHIA C
BUSCHMATTOX AMY LEWIS
BEZZINI MARIO S
ORITZ MIGUEL RICARDO EDWARDO
FUJITA SUMIO
ORITZ MERCEDES JOAQUINA
ROZENTHALL THOMAS T DR
HALSTROM R K
CASQUEZ JUANITA CARMEN
CARRERA ADOLFO
SMITH G WASHINGTON
HILLDOWNING A J
ALSAGE ROBERT F
SAVAGE ERIN P

Exercise 6, Proofreading Your Listing, Page 13

ALLEN JOEL P LT
ALSAGE ROBERT F
ALSHAMMARI FALEH MOHAMMED
BEZZINI MARIO S
BUSCHMATTOX AMY LEWIS
CARRERA ADOLFO
CASQUEZ JUANITA CARMEN

FUJITA SUMIO
FULLER JAMES P
GREENSFELT STEVEN M
HALSTROM R K
HANCOCK PETER M
HILL DOUGLAS J
HILLDOWNING A J
KIM CHEE WON
KIMBELL CYNTHIA C
LABBIE JENNIFER LYNN
MANUEL ROBERTO F
MCMICHAEL MARTIN G
ORITZ MERCEDES JOAQUINA
ORITZ MIGUEL RICARDO EDWARDO
POPEK LEON W
PROSKE SARAH L
ROTHBARRE SERENA K
ROZENTHALL THOMAS T DR
SANDERS JERON P
SAVAGE ERIN P
SHELLEY D SANDERS
SHELTON WILLIAM EDWARD
SMITH G WASHINGTON
SMITH GEORGE W
STJAMES SANDRA T
TAYLOR T DALTON
VANHORN COLLEEN T
WRIGHT PAUL LYNN
ZIMMERMAN JOSEPH J

Unit 3

Exercise 50C, Optional Indexing Exercise, Page 75

0007 SEAS PUBLISHING CO INC
WORD TECHNOLOGY INC
0076 TROMBONES MUSIC STORES THE
TROPEZ TANNING SALON
TRAVELERS INNS INC
SUZZETTES SCHOOL
0010 20 AUTOMOTIVE SUPPLY CO
WORDEX CORP
SILVERTRON ELECTRONICS
WRG FM 96
US GOV INTERIOR DEPARTMENT OF
US GOV EDUCATION DEPARTMENT OF
6001 PEARSON PLACE CLOTHING OUTLETS
VALUE PLUS DRUG STORES
2001 TECHNOLOGIES INC
VARNER RESEARCH CENTER
S AND T HARDWARE
WORDESIGN INC
VAN TECH INC

VIP SALES
R AND R TRAVEL SERVICE INC
Y H WILDER AND SONS
0002 A NOVELTIES
TRUST HELP LINE
0003 M SUPPLY CO
TRAVELERS HELP
US GOV POSTAL SERVICE
WAR AGAINST CANCER
TARGET MS
WAKE CO MANUFACTURING
SAXTON DISTRIBUTORS
0003 WAY DEPARTMENT STORES
UNCLE PETES PLACE
THURSTON ENTERPRISES
SERV N GO DRIVE INS
US GOV INTERNAL REVENUE SERVICE
TOUR AMERICA BUS LINES
S AND N STORES INC
R T STANLEY MANUFACTURERS
WESLEY DISTRIBUTORS
WXTP AM FM
SILVERTRON MINING CO
W B WALKER AND SONS INC
WILLIAMS WAREHOUSES INC
VIVIANS SUNDRIES INC
SMORES BAKERY INC
0003 HOUR LAUNDRY
SAFE WAY THE
TECHNI COMP
REST STOP RESTAURANT THE
WEST COAST HARDWARE SUPPLIES
WEST COAST DEPARTMENT STORES INC
TINY TOTS DAY CARE CENTERS
VERONA LUMBER CO
TYKES CENTERS OF AMERICA
STOCKTON DAIRIES

Exercise 55, Key of Indexed Names, Page 78

0002 A NOVELTIES
0003 HOUR LAUNDRY
0003 M SUPPLY CO
0003 WAY DEPARTMENT STORES
0007 SEAS PUBLISHING CO INC
0010 20 AUTOMOTIVE SUPPLY CO
0076 TROMBONES MUSIC STORES THE
2001 TECHNOLOGIES INC
6001 PEARSON PLACE CLOTHING OUTLETS
R AND R TRAVEL SERVICE INC
R T STANLEY MANUFACTURERS
REST STOP RESTAURANT THE
S AND N STORES INC
S AND T HARDWARE
SAFE WAY THE
SAXTON DISTRIBUTORS
SERV N GO DRIVE INS
SILVERTRON ELECTRONICS
SILVERTRON MINING CO
SMORES BAKERY INC
STOCKTON DAIRIES
SUZZETTES SCHOOL
TARGET MS
TECHNI COMP

THURSTON ENTERPRISES
TINY TOTS DAY CARE CENTERS
TOUR AMERICA BUS LINES
TRAVELERS HELP
TRAVELERS INNS INC
TROPEZ TANNING SALON
TRUST HELP LINE
TYKES CENTERS OF AMERICA
UNCLE PETES PLACE
US GOV EDUCATION DEPARTMENT OF
US GOV INTERIOR DEPARTMENT OF
US GOV INTERNAL REVENUE SERVICE
US GOV POSTAL SERVICE
VALUE PLUS DRUG STORES
VAN TECH INC
VARNER RESEARCH CENTER
VERONA LUMBER CO
VIP SALES
VIVIANS SUNDRIES INC
W B WALKER AND SONS INC
WAKE CO MANUFACTURING
WAR AGAINST CANCER
WESLEY DISTRIBUTORS
WEST COAST DEPARTMENT STORES INC
WEST COAST HARDWARE SUPPLIES
WILLIAMS WAREHOUSES INC
WORD TECHNOLOGY INC
WORDESIGN INC
WORDEX CORP
WRG FM 96
WXTP AM FM
Y H WILDER AND SONS

Exercise 75B, Optional Exercises in Indexing and Data Entry, Page 88

VANNESSAS COSMETICS
RED CROSS THE
SERV N SAVE
T J INVESTMENTS INC
US GOV POSTAL SERVICE
WTQR TV
WONDRA HEALTH SPAS INC
TAX CONSULTANTS UNLIMITED
REST EZ WATERBEDS
OREGON MOTOR VEHICLES DIVISION OF
VERY ONE GIFTS THE
ROGERSPERKINS FUNERAL HOMES
SALVATION TABERNACLE
WOMANS CLUBS OF AMERICA
SAFEGUARDS UNLIMITED
TROUBLE HELP LINE
ROPER INDUSTRIES
US GOV FEDERAL BANKRUPTCY COURT
ROMAN SPAS INC
US GOV COURT HOUSE
SEATTLE VOCATIONAL TRAINING CTR
SEASHORE NATIONAL BANK
US GOV INTERIOR DEPARTMENT OF
VIDEO VUE
VARNER TRUCKING CO
UNDERWOOD GARMENTS INC
THOMAS REED STORES INC
WILLIAMS GROUP THE